THE COLLABORATION BREAKTHROUGH

T0163807

"Collaboration... today's complex, ever-changing, global workplaces. This book provides the essential steps for making it happen."

Naomi Whittel
Chief Executive Officer Reserveage Nutrition and featured on the QVC Shopping Network

"Take a walk in Mike's shoes and you'll be glad you did! Understanding your workplace colleagues, to engage them, to create and build with them, this is what helps ensure success in business and this is what *The Collaboration Breakthrough* will teach you."

Ed Killeen
Chief Operating Officer Uncle Bob's Self Storage

"An executive team must set the example for collaboration in their organization. *The Collaboration Breakthrough* is a toolkit for every leader."

David J. Nasca
President & Chief Executive Officer Evans Bank, N.A.

"When collaboration fails, entire companies rot slowly from fractious conflict. This book does more than describe an idyllic workplace. It walks us step-by-step towards growing trust and effective communication on teams."

Greg Harris
Chief Executive Officer Quantum Workplace & Best Places to Work™ Contest

"*The Collaboration Breakthrough* is an entertaining and insightful guide for solving important and difficult issues faced in today's workplace."

Jamie Latiano Jacobs
Vice President People and Culture, Renovate America and
Vice President, National Human Resources Association

"*The Collaboration Breakthrough* is an incredible resource to identify and priortize action items to influence change in any organization."

Christie Joseph
Vice President of Human Resources, Pegula Sports and Entertainment,
Buffalo Bills and Buffalo Sabres

"In every company there is an unwritten undercurrent of how work gets done. This undercurrent is simply 'collaboration'; and when done effectively it is a key differentiator for any company in any industry. *The Collaboration Breakthrough* is the book that finally gives professionals the insight needed to be exceptional collaborators both at work and in everyday life."

Joshua White
Vice President Learning and Organizational Development, Simon

"It's amazing how impactful Amy can be by keeping things simple and making it easy for people to understand how to be effective with each other and to personally influence organizational effectiveness."

Eugenio Perrier
Chief Marketing Officer, Sabra Dipping Company

"The Collaboration Breakthrough was the perfect next step for our managerial training program."

Kelli Hennessy
Director, Organizational Development and Training, University at Buffalo

"Collaboration will create a workplace with confident employees that trust one another."

Anna Marie Cellino
President National Fuel Gas Distribution Corporation

"The Collaboration Breakthrough gives anyone at any level the confidence and courage to improve the way they work with their co-workers and the results that they deliver."

Jeff Streb
Director of Human Resources, US Technology Solutions, Ingram Micro Inc.

"This step-by-step guide provides a simple framework for making collaboration the cornerstone of your company culture."

David Rendall
Author of *The Freak Factor*

THE
COLLABORATION
BREAKTHROUGH

THE
COLLABORATION
BREAKTHROUGH

Think differently. *Achieve more.*

AMY A. PEARL

Advantage®

Published by Advantage, Charleston, South Carolina.
Member of Advantage Media Group.

ADVANTAGE is a registered trademark and the Advantage colophon is a trademark of Advantage Media Group, Inc.

Printed in the United States of America.

ISBN: 978-1-64225-183-8
LCCN: 2020905302

Book design by George Stevens

This publication is designed to provide accurate and authoritative information in regard to the subject matter covered. It is sold with the understanding that the publisher is not engaged in rendering legal, accounting, or other professional services. If legal advice or other expert assistance is required, the services of a competent professional person should be sought.

Advantage Media Group is proud to be a part of the Tree Neutral® program. Tree Neutral offsets the number of trees consumed in the production and printing of this book by taking proactive steps such as planting trees in direct proportion to the number of trees used to print books. To learn more about Tree Neutral, please visit **www.treeneutral.com**. To learn more about Advantage's commitment to being a responsible steward of the environment, please visit **www.advantagefamily.com/green**

Advantage Media Group is a publisher of business, self-improvement, and professional development books and online learning. We help entrepreneurs, business leaders, and professionals share their Stories, Passion, and Knowledge to help others Learn & Grow. Do you have a manuscript or book idea that you would like us to consider for publishing? Please visit **advantagefamily.com** or call **1.866.775.1696.**

For Michael and Grace,

*May you always find Collaborative Workplaces
or have the courage to create them!*

THE COLLABORATION BREAKTHROUGH

8304 Main Street

Williamsville, New York 14221

www.CollaborationBreakthrough.com

Table of Contents

INTRODUCTION

The Case for Collaboration

*Any fool can make things complex. It takes
a genius to make something simple.*

We get it ... you're tired. Trying to keep all those balls in the air is simply exhausting. Today's workplace is more complex than ever. Getting products to market is complicated by challenges with few single causes or simple solutions. A steady stream of new technologies creates big changes every day. You work across unfamiliar cultures and inconvenient time zones. And, if that weren't enough, volatile economic conditions have made predicting the future nearly impossible.

You juggle demands from customers, bosses, peers, direct reports, and others who often don't agree with each other or have the patience to wait. With all of the distractions and priorities, it's difficult to get your most important work accomplished. You work too much, yet you still don't have enough time for creative thinking and innovation. And you don't feel appreciated, which makes sense because what you do doesn't seem to make much of a difference anyway. Sometimes you may be thankful that you just survived another week.

To push ahead, businesses use agile development, big data, ERP systems, matrix management, and open office spaces—tactics that are designed to make work easier but actually make life more complicated. Hierarchical or matrix reporting structures hamper innovation, teamwork, accountability, and results. And despite an abundance of training programs designed to get "millennials" to be "disruptors" and "synergize" their "it factors" to drive "engagement," buzzword programs have only created more complexity and more work. No wonder you're more stretched and stressed than ever before.

Oddly enough, a simple answer has always been right in front of you. Regardless of all the changes taking place in organizations, one thing remains constant: the *people* who work there. Around the world, in all kinds of workplaces, you and other talented, passionate people show up each day, wanting to be successful and wanting to feel fulfilled. Your goals? To make progress, enjoy what you do, be treated fairly, learn and grow, and take pride in your work.

THERE IS A BRIGHT SIDE

Organizations that weather economic storms, come first to market with new ideas and approaches, grow a satisfied customer base, and excel financially have found the solution is really quite simple. Imagine for a moment, a workplace where

- you and your coworkers share a clear and common purpose;

- you have open and respectful conversations;

- you can easily build commitment to new ideas and ways of doing things;

- simple tools and processes guide decisions, actions, and accountability;

- each day provides opportunities to learn and grow; and

- you and your coworkers have complete trust and confidence in one another.

What would life be like? Would you achieve your goals? Would customers and partners become enthusiastic and loyal fans? Would you crush your competition? Would you feel your own personal level of ownership increase? Would you and your coworkers be skipping to work? We think so. In fact, we know so.

This workplace exists. We call it a Collaborative Workplace, a workplace where simple tools and common-sense frameworks invite people to make things happen. In a Collaborative Workplace people think differently and achieve more.

IF IT'S SO SIMPLE, WHY ISN'T EVERYONE DOING IT?

For starters, collaboration seems hard to measure. "Touchy-feely" might be how some executives see it. To them, traditional, quantifiable measures of success are more reliable. Yet, study after study shows CEOs often worry most about people problems.

Building collaboration also takes a consistent, long-term approach. Contrast that with tactical actions—say a marketing campaign or a training program that can be short-term and flexible. Like any kind of fitness program, creating a Collaborative Workplace takes discipline. This is not a mugs and posters program; it's a way of life.

Perhaps the biggest reason people don't collaborate is it requires facing the realities of human behavior, behavior that even the most committed people find difficult to comprehend, let alone address. Instead, they wait for their boss, the CEO, or the board of directors to deal with the tough issues when, in reality, every person has the power to influence others to build a better workplace—a Collaborative Workplace. This is the collaboration breakthrough. It's a shift in your thinking that drives a better approach to how you work with others.

We've spent the past 20 years studying collaboration in the workplace. We've worked in and with some of the most dysfunctional workplaces and some of the most amazing workplaces. We've surveyed thousands of workers to understand their challenges and ideas for creating more collaboration. And in our quest to provide strategic solutions and simple tools, our clients have grown their organizations, launched new products faster than ever before, implemented sweeping changes with less pain, expedited merger and acquisition processes, and won awards as industry leaders. Their employees don't quit (mentally or literally), and the number and quality of applicants interested in joining them soars.

One of the most compelling results came from our client, John, a chief operating officer of a large health system. In a January coaching session, John shared their many successes of the prior year: new service lines, better quality, more satisfied patients. For the first time in many years, they hit their profit targets. When asked what drove this success, John replied, "It's simple. We're just treating people better. We're thinking differently about our team members, and that's affecting the decisions we make and the results we achieve. We work together to make the changes we all want to see in health care."

John's right. It's as simple as that.

The collaboration breakthrough isn't complicated at all, and this book will show you how to achieve it.

LET'S HAVE SOME FUN

We've written this book in a way that we hope you'll find entertaining. You'll meet Mike Learner, a bright (almost fictitious) finance grad who has just started his first job as an accountant at an (almost fictitious) manufacturing firm. You'll walk alongside Mike as he experiences four different workplaces and the collaboration breakthrough. You'll likely recognize your current workplace among them and also identify which one you'd *like* to have. We're confident you'll choose the Collaborative Workplace, so in part two we give you the hands-on tools and additional information you need to make the shift on your own, wherever you are and regardless of your job title.

As you're about to learn, creating the collaboration break-through is not only doable, it's essential in today's highly chaotic, competitive, uncertain, and ever-changing business landscape. The only question is:

Do you have the courage to make it happen?

PART ONE

THE FABLE

The Dream Workplace

The Collaborative Workplace: The more people know, the more they can contribute.

Hey, it's nice to meet you! I'm Mike Learner, and I work in the finance department at Lakeside Manufacturing. I've been with Lakeside for six months now, and I absolutely love it. This is my first job out of college, and I feel as if I hit the cool job lottery. This company is the perfect fit for me, and I have a feeling Lakeside feels the same way. The HR manager said they hired me because I demonstrated respect, responsibility, and results in college and in my prior jobs. Respect, responsibility, and results, or the "Three Rs" as they're referred to around here, aren't just some meaningless catchphrase. From what I can see, our executive team and managers demonstrate them in everything they say and do, and they expect all of us to carry them out as well. That's not hard to do when everyone around me is so positive and focused on our shared goals. I know it sounds like a cliché, but we really do operate like a well-oiled machine here.

My first three months at Lakeside were a whirlwind of meetings with executives, managers, and employees at every level. It was fun getting acquainted with everyone; they seemed genuinely happy to welcome me aboard and to get to know me too. During my first three months on the job, I spent a week in every department so I could begin to understand how each one contributes to Lakeside's success and to get to know people across the organization. I also participated in weekly training sessions to learn the company's core processes. Every day was a revelation for me. It was like walking through a real-world primer on how to run a business where people have confidence in one another and produce excellent results together.

TEAM CIRCLES KEEP US CONNECTED AND FOCUSED

I quickly learned that there are routines at Lakeside designed to get us all rowing in the same direction. As the former captain of my college crew team, I know how important this is. For example, first thing every Monday morning, we have a meeting known as Team Circle. It's not only called a circle because we sit in a circle but also because there is no hierarchy in these meetings. We're all equal regardless of our position and tenure. How many business teams can say that about their meetings? Not very many, based on what I hear from my college buddies who work in other jobs. One of my friends told me that she thinks she ages at ten times the normal rate during her company's meetings, and I don't think she was kidding when she said that. At Lakeside we don't use a conference room or anything that formal when we get together. We just pull our chairs into a circle. The chairs don't even match. One is trendy and stylish. One is a traditional wooden chair like you'd find in your grandmother's attic. One is bold and large. The funny thing is I sort of feel like the chairs actually match the personalities of my eclectic team members.

Our Team Circle is guided by Ann, our team captain. Ann was appointed to serve in this role for one year because she is really good at getting teams excited about their work. Job rotations are frequent at Lakeside because changing roles is a great way to learn new things while walking a mile in someone else's shoes. The team captain position is no exception; it rotates every 12 to 18 months. Team captains are chosen based on their personal career goals, positive feedback from coworkers, and how well they inspire the company's values in others. Ann launches each Team Circle by reminding us of our three most important goals for the quarter. Right now, our "big three" are to (1) sell $2 million in product, (2) achieve 98 percent on-time delivery, and (3) implement the next modules of our new automated accounting system. It might seem odd to begin a finance team meeting with goals having to do with sales and on-time delivery, but at Lakeside, the same "big three" goals apply to every person in every department. Each of us is clear on what the goals are and how we contribute to them.

After Ann reminds us of the "big three," my five peers and I each have three minutes to update the group on the previous week's accomplishments and this week's plan. Everyone is prepared because the agenda seldom varies. This sort of consistency keeps everyone on the same page. Our favorite part of Team Circle is when we vote on who gets to keep the team trophy on their desk that week. We choose these people because they've done something that brought us one step closer to a "big three" goal or because they've done something that demonstrated one or more of the Three Rs. All of our most critical goals and values are constantly reinforced. It's awesome!

I know I'm making it sound as if everything's always perfect at Lakeside, but the truth is we have problems just as every business does. The difference is that we actively deal with our problems as a team rather than trying to pretend they're not there or trying to pass them off to someone else.

In our last Team Circle, my coworker Steve announced, "Houston, we have a problem!" The rest of us simultaneously shouted in response, "Let's tackle it!"

Now, I have to admit that this ritual seemed counterintuitive the first time I witnessed it. My business school professors had taught me to think deeply about threats and challenges and try to resolve them myself as best I could. The rationale was that you had to be a smart, independent thinker and solve your own problems. But at Lakeside, employees are encouraged to come right out and tell people about problems as soon as they spot them. When a coworker cites a challenge and we respond with a rousing "Let's tackle it!", that's our way of saying we're all here to help. We're all in this together because we share common goals. Here people can admit their mistakes, struggles, and weaknesses and know without a doubt that they'll have the full support of their team.

Back to Steve and his problem: Steve is responsible for publishing the company's sales and profitability forecasts, but to do so, he must get numbers from the sales department, and those numbers don't always come on time. Steve fears that another delay will occur this month and our finance team will look bad. Ann promised that Steve's concern would be addressed the next day in the weekly problem-solving meeting. Steve will be required to attend and so will Dan, since he is the sales liaison for our finance team. Their work is directly impacted by the problem. All other team members are invited if they have ideas or would like to be part of the discussion. After all, the whole point of having a Collaborative Workplace is to allow everyone to bring their talents and best ideas to the table to solve problems and get stuff done. Ann wraps up each thirty-minute Team Circle with our **agreement-building questions**:

- What did we decide today?

- Who is going to do what? By when?

- Who needs to know about this?

- What is the message and the tone of that message?

The agreement-building questions help each of us be personally accountable for our responsibilities and ensure that people who aren't at Team Circle are kept in the loop. Before we walk away, Ann encourages us to keep talking and sharing information by reminding us that *the more people know, the more they can contribute.*

DAILY DRIVE-BYS KEEP THE LINES OF COMMUNICATION OPEN

Ann's support doesn't begin and end at Team Circle. Almost every day she stops by my desk for a quick chat—a visit she calls a drive-by. Ann doesn't only do drive-bys with me. She checks in with everyone on the team, and she always starts by asking us the same question:

Do you have everything you need to achieve great results today?

This morning when Ann came to my desk, I told her that I needed to talk to her about a sticky problem I've been having with a certain section of the financial report that I'm responsible for completing each month. As always, when one of us has a problem or concern, Ann responds with three questions that are designed to get us to a solution quickly and efficiently. She calls this line of questioning **Coaching Conversations.**

"Okay, tell me about the problem," Ann said.

"Well, I'm not satisfied with the look of the *Cost of Goods Sold* report," I replied. "There's a lot of room for improvement. It's confusing to read, and people don't understand it, so I end up fielding a lot of questions every month. It's not very user-friendly in its current format."

Ann nodded. "What would you like the report to look like?"

"Simple, streamlined, and easy to read. Some graphs would be great too."

"And how do you think you can make that happen?"

"I'm certain that with a little work, I can create a new format that will really help. If it works the way I believe it will, it should save a lot of time and help people understand our financials so they can make better decisions. I'd like to give it a try this month and see if it works. It should only take me a day or two. Would that be okay?"

"Of course. Have at it," she said. "I want to thank you for challenging the way we do things and for being so innovative. I have complete faith in you, so by all means, give it a shot."

I won't be surprised if Ann celebrates my idea at next Monday's Team Circle. But I *was* surprised at what she said next …

"Now I need your help, Mike," she said. "In my last 360 degree feedback report, I discovered that my listening skills could use some improvement, and I've been working hard on that. I appreciate your candor, so I'd like your honest feedback on how I'm doing so far. Would you please give me some specific examples of situations in which I could have listened more, along with some examples of times I listened well? Again, you are free to be 100 percent honest with me here."

Wow. A supervisor asking a rookie like me for my opinion of her job performance? While it was easy for me to tell Ann about the times I've seen her do well, I didn't quite feel comfortable sharing critical feedback. What if I said something that offended her? What if she decided to hold it against me? She's my supervisor; she could make my life a living hell if she wanted to. But Ann seemed so sincere and open to hearing my thoughts that I decided to trust her and tell her my views. I'm glad I did, because it seemed to please her. She didn't become defensive. She actually thanked me for my candor and reminded me that she values my opinion and feedback very much. She invited me to always tell her what I think.

Next, Ann asked me if I have everything I need for my monthly coaching meeting with my senior mentor, Carlos, who is Lakeside's VP of operations. I reassured her that I was all set. I look forward to my meetings with Carlos because they give me an opportunity to learn more about all aspects of our organization and to network with some influential people in the company. As Carlos always says, "If you want to be successful in work and in life, you have to surround yourself with successful people." That's not hard to do at Lakeside; there's certainly no shortage of successful people around here!

THE WAKE-UP CALL

At Tuesday's problem-solving meeting, we tackled Steve's concern by following our structured problem-solving process. Steve restated his problem, and then we all began offering our ideas for fixing it. Whenever one of us makes a suggestion in a problem-solving meeting, we can always count on Dan, our team skeptic, to bring up at least three potential obstacles. Dan has a reputation for being the "no guy" in our group, but we all appreciate how great he is at seeing things that might go wrong in any given situation. His track record for keeping our team out of trouble is impressive, so we respect his opinions and his wisdom. This particular meeting was no exception. Dan pointed out a couple of flaws in the idea I put forth, but I didn't take it personally. Dan was respectful when delivering his critique, and he was right. The team simply moved on, generating lots of ideas and then prioritizing them based on their impact on the goal and the effort we'd need to execute them. During these meetings we set our egos aside, stay focused, and refuse to give up. And, as usual, we were able to arrive at a decision on the most effective ways to solve Steve's problem and actions. To make sure we all agreed with the action plan, we used the same **agreement-building questions** that Ann had used at Team Circle:

- What did we decide today?

- Who is going to do what? By when?

- Who needs to know about this?

- What is the message and the tone of that message?

At the next weekly Team Circle the camaraderie, enthusiasm, and trust in the room were energizing. I was so excited to be a part of this team. I was learning so much, and I felt that I was really contributing. As always, Ann kicked things off by reminding us of our "big three" quarterly business goals and the Three Rs. To celebrate my *Cost of Goods Sold* report improvements and the team's winning solution to Steve's problem, Ann rang a bell. She started out ringing it softly, but then she began ringing it louder… and louder…and *louder*.

Wait…that's not the sound of Ann ringing a bell; it's my alarm clock. Lakeside was only a dream! Today is my first day on the job at the *real* Lakeside Manufacturing. I can't wait.

CHAPTER 2

The Nightmare— The Defensive Workplace

The less said, the better.

I was excited to dive into my new job, so on my first day I got there a few minutes early. I'd been instructed to stop by human resources to fill out the required payroll and benefits paperwork, but when I arrived, the guy in the lobby told me that Shelly, the vice president of human resources, had been called to an emergency meeting. He didn't know what the meeting was about or how long it would last, so he told me to take a seat.

Shelly appeared about 30 minutes later with a harried apology for keeping me waiting. We went over all of the paperwork she had for me to sign, and she handed me my access card to the building. She gave me a quick lesson on how to use the time clock, and then she escorted me to my desk. Shelly was actually a little scary.

I think the best word to describe my grey, fabric-covered cubicle was "sterile." The artificial lighting was super bright and harsh. There was one piece of artwork hanging behind my desk, a calendar with a black-and-white photo of Mount Everest on it. Dark-grey industrial carpeting covered the floor with stark white walls all around. On my desk was a tall stack of manuals.

"Your manager, Todd, will be here shortly," Shelly said curtly. "He'll take you around and introduce you to your direct-report team and then treat you to lunch. In the meantime, you can start reading through these manuals. Let me know if you have any questions, okay? Welcome aboard and good luck!"

I thanked Shelly for her time and sat down at my desk. The *Lakeside Employee Handbook* was at the top of the pile of manuals, so I started with that one. It was full of legal stuff and technical jargon, and it was quite long and complicated for a handbook. Still, I managed to take away some important points after reading it:

O   Lakeside has a strict "business professional" dress code for office workers.

O   No snacks or lunches may be eaten at your desk.

O   Work areas must be kept free of clutter, such as family photos and plants.

○　No moving the furniture around.

○　No music or "boisterous talking" allowed.

○　Senior management approval is required for a lot of things, such as taking a day off or giving a customer something more than what is in the contract.

It looks as if Lakeside runs a tight ship! Thankfully, my new boss, Todd, the VP of finance, arrived at noon to take me to lunch, giving me a welcome break from my reading.

LUNCH WITH TODD

Todd seemed like a nice enough guy. He's about 15 years older than me, and he's been with Lakeside for ten years. On our short walk to the deli down the street, he told me that he has a wife who's a nurse, three kids under the age of seven, a golden retriever, and a chronic case of acid reflux, which he attributes to "all the damn stress." Over Buffalo chicken wings he told me about our general manager, Dr. Right, who had recently been promoted from the corporate research and development team.

"We were really excited about working with Dr. Right because he's like a rock star in the industry," Todd said. "The guy's brilliant. He has a PhD in chemistry, and his work has led to several advancements in our field. Our parent company supports promotion from within, so we weren't exactly shocked that they sent us Dr. Right even though he's never served in a leadership role."

It was cool that Lakeside's executive team was willing to put an inexperienced manager into a GM position. *Hey,* I thought, *maybe I'll be able to climb the corporate ladder too!*

Todd went on to explain that the team's excitement over Dr. Right's arrival was short-lived. According to Todd, Dr. Right's quirks and lack of people skills quickly revealed themselves.

"Dr. Right is very precise in everything he says and does. He looks like he just walked off the pages of *Popular Science* magazine. He still wears his starched white lab coat, complete with pocket protector, even though he's rarely in the lab anymore. Even his posture is ramrod straight," Todd explained. "He's somewhat pessimistic and high strung, and he's got this 'I'm smarter than you' leadership style, which can be kind of intimidating. We're never sure what he wants, so we just do our best to focus on what we think is important. He's very critical too, but don't take anything he says to heart. It's nothing personal. He treats all of us the same lousy way."

Todd continued, "Oh, and one last thing, Dr. Right always works with his door closed. He's a very private person. Whatever you do, don't knock on that door, man…unless the building is on fire or the Messiah has just walked into the lobby."

By the time lunch was over, I was pretty sure the work environment at the real Lakeside was going to be a far cry from my dream. Turns out I was right. Over the first few months on the job, I was surprised to discover that

O   There are no team meetings—ever.

- Dr. Right makes all the decisions, and he appears to be obsessed with details about strange things, such as chart colors.

- No one talks about common goals, roles, or accomplishments. In fact, it seems the only things people are interested in doing are fighting for their own objectives and protecting their turf, if they really even care at all.

- There are many problems, but no one owns them. There's constant blame and finger pointing and a ton of ugly gossip. Everyone is constantly on the defensive. You never know if you're going to be the next one under attack or the next one blamed for something that's gone wrong.

- Dr. Right operates on a need-to-know basis. Even though I graduated with a master's degree in accounting and have been hired to do this job in the finance department, I'm not given the information it takes to really understand our organization's total financial picture.

- People are quitting left and right. We are always hearing rumors that someone is thinking of leaving.

I admit that I too was tempted to quit several times, but I grew to like my team of direct reports a lot. I didn't want to abandon them, so I stayed. And for some unknown reason, I still had hope that things would improve. I wanted to play an active role in bringing about that improvement, but I had no idea how to start. The only thing I knew for sure was that any improvement efforts would require working with (or around) Dr. Right…and that was much easier said than done.

WISDOM FROM AN UNLIKELY SOURCE

One night, I was working late at the office, trying to get a report done because, as usual, Dr. Right had dictated an order about something he wanted, and the deadline was the next day. It was so frustrating. I was the only one on our team who ever put in extra time, so I was alone. The office was always a ghost town after five o'clock.

I was sitting at my desk, wrestling with some numbers, when I heard someone open the outer office door. It was Marty from the mailroom, whistling a happy tune as he made his nightly rounds.

"Hello, Mike!" Marty said. "What in the world are you doing here at this hour? Most people book out of here at four forty-five!"

Marty's one of those people you can't help but like. He's always got a smile on his face and a friendly greeting whenever I see him. Marty could have retired a long time ago, but he decided against it. "I like to stay busy," he once told me. "Why should I sit home alone when I can come here, visit with all of you, *and* collect a paycheck? Keeps me young, this place."

For someone in his late 70s, Marty's got a lot of energy. He's also got a lot of life experience and wisdom.

"I'm sure you don't want to hear my problems," I said.

"Nonsense," Marty said as he pulled up a chair. "You and I are on the same team. I'm happy to listen to what you have to say."

"I'm here at this hour because I'm busting my butt to finish a report that's due tomorrow. It wasn't finished before now because Dr. Right just decided what he wanted at the last minute. *Again*. Nobody else on the team is even interested in working to fix the report. So here I am, doing it all myself."

Marty nodded. It felt good to have someone who seemed to care.

"I'm just so discouraged. Hell, we all are," I continued, feeling myself becoming more heated. "None of us knows how to function under Dr. Right's leadership—if you can call it that. It seems like he only sticks his head out from behind the curtain to hand down a list of demands or to pull the rug out from under us!"

"Okay, hold on now," Marty said. "Take a deep breath. You have a lot going on. Let me ask you a question. **What's the most difficult or important issue you have to deal with right now?**"

"Right now, I have to get this report done."

"I don't think so, Mike," Marty interrupted. "That sounds like your most urgent problem. What I asked was, 'What's the most difficult or important issue you have to deal with right now?'"

I thought for a moment. "Well, if you put it that way, right now I want to have an honest conversation with Dr. Right about the way things are around here, but Todd warned me that I shouldn't even try."

"Well," Marty replied, "**Why would Dr. Right want to talk to you?**" He leaned back in his chair, waiting for my answer.

"Because my team and I have some ideas that would help make things better. Take this report for example. If I had access to the right data at the right time, this would take much less effort and would probably save the company money too."

"That sounds like something he'd be interested in hearing," Marty said. "But the challenge comes in making yourself heard. **How do you speak his language so that your voice is heard?**"

"How do I speak *his* language? What is *his* language?"

"To speak someone's language simply means that you use words they can understand and relate to," Marty replied. "You meet him where he's at. You get his attention by addressing his priorities. So what words would Dr. Right relate to? What are his priorities?"

I thought about that for a minute. Then I got out a sheet of paper and a pen so I could make a list of all the things I knew for sure about Dr. Right. My mom always told me, "if you want to change the world, you first need to change your thinking." Maybe I'm looking at Dr. Right all wrong. Maybe I needed to turn my negative feelings about Dr. Right into positives in order to see what's important to him. For example, rather than writing that Dr. Right is *aloof* or *unwilling to share information with us*, I'd describe him as *quiet* and *reserved*. Here's the list I came up with:

DR. RIGHT

- ✓ Quiet, reserved, likes to think
- ✓ Values accuracy and quality
- ✓ Highly analytical
- ✓ Likes facts and data/doesn't like assumptions
- ✓ Has a lot of expertise in our field
- ✓ Has high standards and asks tough questions so we achieve them
- ✓ Conscientious

I reviewed my list and thought about what it meant. It wasn't long before I had an epiphany. *Dr. Right is so critical and demanding because he's afraid to fail or to even make a mistake. In fact, he probably worries a lot about all of us failing on his watch.*

"Since Dr. Right fears failure and values quality, analysis, and knowledge so much, I would have to use those words if I approached him with my ideas," I said. "That's how I speak his language and prove to him that I respect his expertise and care about quality too. I need to show him the risk of failure with me is very slight because I'm competent and reliable. That's the way to earn Dr. Right's trust and confidence. That's the way to get him to hear me out and listen to my ideas!"

I could actually hear the frustration in my voice turning to optimism.

"But I can't just spring something on him out of the blue," I continued, thinking aloud. "I have to go about this in a way that respects his position and his reserved nature. I know, I'll schedule a formal appointment to share the data I've been gathering."

"Well then," Marty said, "it sounds like you've had a breakthrough. You know what you need to do and why you're the best person for the job."

"I sure hope so, Marty. I have no idea how he's going to react, though. What if he throws me out?"

"Don't you think that's a chance worth taking? Look at how miserable you are now. Honestly, **what have you got to lose?**"

Marty's question stopped me in my tracks. The look on my face must have been priceless, because Marty tossed back his head and laughed out loud.

"Better get back to work," Marty said, pushing back from my desk and standing. "But before I go, there's one more thing I want to tell you: Everything you need to be successful is right here, so go for it."

I thought about Marty's questions as I watched him stroll out the door whistling. *Why would Dr. Right want to talk to me? I suppose he would only want to talk to me if he thought I knew what's important to him. That I "get" him. That I understand his priorities and preferences, and I communicate with him in a way that reinforces his way of looking at and being in the world.*

Problem was I didn't meet that description—at least not yet. But I knew that I could if I put some thought and effort into it. As Marty pointed out, what did I have to lose?

As I drove home later that night I recalled my dream workplace. I vowed to establish as many elements of that collaborative spirit as I could at the real Lakeside despite the constraints. I became determined to confront Dr. Right to try to make a difference.

WINNING MINDS, THEN HEARTS

A few days later I ran into Dr. Right in the hallway, and I was ready for him.

"Excuse me, Dr. Right," I said as we approached one another.

"Yes, what is it? I have a conference call in three minutes …"

"This will take less than 60 seconds. I just read the article you published in the industry journal last month. It was excellent. I learned a lot from it."

I thought I detected the tiniest sliver of a smile crossing Dr. Right's face. I pushed onward.

"Sir, I've been thinking. In preparing the on-time delivery report you asked for earlier this week, it occurred to me that if I had access to the right data I could incorporate it into my report. This would give you more insight and help you in your decision making. May I ask your permission to schedule an appointment with you later this week to show you some of my data? I'll even send you a sample report this afternoon so you can take a look."

Dr. Right gave me a curt nod. "Yes, call Denise to schedule the meeting. What's your name again?"

"I'm Mike Learner from Finance. I look forward to our meeting, Dr. Right. I promise I won't waste your time."

And so I was able to open the proverbial door to Dr. Right's psyche, if only just a crack. We had our meeting later that week, and it went very well. Over the next few weeks I did everything I could think of to boost my team's credibility with Dr. Right (without going overboard, of course). Initially, I was worried about stepping on Todd's toes since he was my manager, and people really get defensive here when you tread on their turf. But he didn't seem to care, so I pressed forward with Dr. Right. All I had to do was demonstrate that he and I valued the same things—that we spoke the same language. Every time I had an idea to improve the quality of our department's work, I presented it to Dr. Right with a strong, logical rationale for why I was sure it would succeed. Once I had his attention and confidence, I was able to get him to listen to my ideas. In fact, it worked so well that he didn't dictate any more last-minute tasks to my team.

Although it wasn't an ideal situation, I stuck with it. The biggest problem for my team was they were used to waiting for orders to come down from Dr. Right. It was almost as if they had stopped thinking for themselves. They had lost their sense of confidence and had no framework for making decisions about what needed to be done. If responsibility is truly one of the Three Rs, we needed to demonstrate that we walked the talk, even if others didn't. We had to show we were competent and reliable and that we really cared about what was important to other people.

Over time my efforts paid off. My small team was given access to a lot of top-secret information that we were able to use to create some great financial analyses and projections for Dr. Right. He really seemed to value our input. Naturally, this made a few people jealous, but I didn't care. I wasn't there to compete. I was there to maintain a positive environment for my team and to do good work. Still, working in survival strategy mode every day was taking its toll. I loved working with my team, but I didn't feel I was collaborating well with my peers. And watching Todd and the other senior managers cower to Dr. Right was getting old.

I recall one particularly difficult day after about two years on the job. I was sitting at my desk, fighting the urge to type up my resignation letter, hand it to Shelly in HR, and walk out the door forever, but I couldn't bear the thought of leaving my team. I needed a miracle—and fast.

At that precise moment an e-mail appeared in my inbox. It was from the corporate director of human resources, and the subject line read "Organizational Change."

CHAPTER 3

Turnover at the Top—The Paternalistic Workplace

We only talk about the good things.

Aaccording to the message from corporate HR, after just three years in the GM role, Dr. Right was being transferred out of the country to explore new research and development partnerships. I didn't fault the parent company for giving the guy a chance to lead. But I was glad they saw he really belonged in a job where he didn't manage anybody. He had made some great contributions to the company, but working with people wasn't his strength. I hoped the next GM could help build our team.

The e-mail went on to announce that our new GM would be Glinda Nurturino. Glinda had managed the marketing department at another facility, Riverfront, before being named GM at Lakeside. So I called Alysha, my friend in the finance department at Riverfront, to get the lowdown on Glinda before her arrival.

"Ah, Glinda Nurturino," Alysha said with a chuckle. "She's a sweet person, no doubt about it. Easygoing, friendly, patient… like your favorite auntie."

"But?" I asked. "Come on, Alysha, there's got to be a 'but' in there somewhere, right?"

"Of course! Nobody's perfect. But I'm going to leave it at that and let you draw your own conclusions about Glinda. It's only fair."

Alysha was right; it was only fair. But after all I'd been through with Dr. Right, can you really blame me for trying to get the advance scoop on our new GM?

A BREATH OF FRESH AIR

Instead of hiding out in her office on her first day at Lakeside, Glinda strolled from desk to desk introducing herself, shaking hands, and engaging in small talk with every member of the department. It was clear within minutes of meeting her that she was much more interested in people than Dr. Right had been. What a welcome relief!

"Mike Learner, I've heard such wonderful things about you," she said as she approached my desk. I stood to shake her hand and was immediately captured by the warmth and sincerity of her smile. Alysha was right; Glinda really did look like your favorite aunt. As we talked about my team and what we were working on, I couldn't help but notice how interested she was in our conversation. It was clear from her body language and facial expressions that she was listening—really listening—and she truly cared about what I had to say. She closed our conversation by stating she had an open-door policy, and I should never hesitate to pop in and chat.

"I'll do that, Ms. Nurturino," I said.

"Oh, please call me Glinda," she replied. "We're family now, for heaven's sake!"

Glinda's first official order of business was to hold a senior leadership team retreat. The other employees and I were not invited, but afterward, we saw signs that interesting things must have happened there. First, Todd returned from the retreat limping, with his ankle wrapped. When we asked him what happened, he snarled and mumbled something about "that freakin' ropes course." We decided to leave it at that.

Next, colorful posters started popping up on the walls touting Lakeside's new mission statement, five-year vision, and six new core values. Glinda launched a monthly newsletter to share information about new customers and industry trends, which was great. She implemented a monthly birthday celebration lunch. We all received 3 percent pay increases and an additional contribution to our health insurance plan. Then she started an Employee of the Month award (although no one was quite sure what we had to do to win it). Scented soaps even appeared in the bathrooms.

Glinda began holding monthly meetings with select employees so they could hang out with her for an hour and ask her questions. She christened these gatherings "Coffee with Glinda." I was invited to one of them. We all sat around a conference table and had (you guessed it) coffee. There was a platter of doughnuts and also a bowl of fruit that Glinda said was for those of us who might be into healthy eating.

"I want to make sure everyone here is totally comfortable and 100 percent happy," Glinda said with a smile as she kicked off the meeting. I remember thinking that if Betty Crocker had been a real person, she would probably have looked and acted exactly like Glinda Nurturino.

Although it was a pleasant gathering, I thought the questions people asked Glinda were pretty safe and superficial. The rumor mill had been running in overdrive lately because of unexplained staff and expense cuts. Employees wondered why the company was spending money on birthday celebrations while workers were losing their jobs. People were beginning to worry about Lakeside's future.

I decided to ask Glinda about the rumor that a new competitor, Gulfstream, was gearing up to challenge us on our turf. If the gossip was true, Lakeside was going to have a fight on its hands, which was upsetting people on my team.

"Now don't you worry about that, Mike," Glinda said. "First of all, Gulfstream has no competitive advantage over us whatsoever, and second, that's what our senior leadership team is for, to look out for challenges in the marketplace so that you and the folks on your team don't have to worry. I assure you there's no reason for you to be concerned. Doughnut, anyone?"

I had hoped Glinda would give us some concrete information about the Gulfstream threat, but for whatever reason, she was choosing not to. As disappointing as that was, I had to admit that people welcomed the changes Glinda had made in her first year at Lakeside. She was much more approachable and easy to talk to than Dr. Right. Still, why did I feel as much in the dark with Glinda at the helm as I had with Dr. Right?

LIMPING OFF INTO THE SUNSET

One day Todd abruptly called the finance team together in the conference room for an impromptu meeting.

"You all know I'm not one to beat around the bush," he said. "I've called you here today to tell you that I've resigned from my post as VP of finance, effective the fifteenth of this month. I've been offered a senior management position with another company, and I'm taking it. I'll stick around for a couple of weeks to help Glinda find my replacement, and then I'm outta here. So that's it. It's been great. You all are awesome. I'm going to miss you. Now, get back to work."

Classic Todd. Sure, he was a little rough around the edges sometimes, but I liked the guy, and I was going to miss him too.

Todd's leaving was certainly a loss for me. But as is true with most things in life, every cloud has a silver lining. In this case, I didn't have to wait long to find the silver lining in Todd's departure. A week after his surprise announcement, I was chosen to take his place as VP of Lakeside's finance department. I was promoted just in time to attend Glinda's second off-site retreat. Todd would be coming along too so he could present the finance report one last time before he left for his new job the next day. He offered to serve as my chauffeur to the meeting.

"It's the least I can do for the new big-shot VP," he said.

I could not have been more excited. My dream of being part of a management team had come true. But I should have been careful what I wished for because what I learned at that retreat with Glinda and my new peer group was shocking.

Renaldo, our VP of sales, announced that we had lost our biggest customer to Gulfstream. Turns out the water cooler rumors were true. The threat from our competitor had been a serious one, despite Glinda's denial at her monthly coffee meeting. *How can this be?* I thought. *We've heard nothing about Gulfstream in the monthly newsletter or at any of the dozens of monthly parties and gatherings we've had since Glinda's arrival. No wonder she never answers the tough questions! Perhaps if we hadn't been kept in the dark, we could have worked together to come up with some customer retention strategies and saved that account.*

Things really got intense when Shelly, the VP of HR, boldly stated, "Well, Renaldo, if you had implemented that sales training program I suggested six months ago, we wouldn't be in this position!"

That set off 45 minutes of heated argument, primarily between Shelly and Renaldo. I kept looking to Glinda, expecting her to step in to help resolve the conflict or at least send Shelly and Renaldo to their respective corners to cool off. But she did nothing. She just sat there with this vacant expression on her face, like a deer caught in the headlights, until Shelly and Renaldo finally ran out of steam. The other team members either looked fed up or just completely disinterested, checking their messages or perhaps playing video games for all I knew. The meeting ended with a resounding thud.

On the drive home, Todd and I talked about the meeting and sorry state of the senior management team.

"After seeing that hot mess, I guess it's clear to you why I'm leaving," Todd said.

"Yeah, wow. That really blew my mind," I said. "I had no idea there was so much animosity among the senior managers. I always thought everyone got along so well. How long has it been like this?"

"Ever since Glinda took over," he replied. "It's crazy. She manages this business like a den mother running a Cub Scout troop. She expects all the kids to behave and get along. Managers are expected to keep everyone happy. She only wants to talk about the good stuff; everything else gets swept under the rug because she doesn't want to upset anybody."

"But as you know, there are no secrets in organizations," Todd continued. "People aren't stupid. They can see that we're not getting as many orders. They can see that we're cutting expenses all over the place, so naturally, they wonder what's going on. Yet

Glinda refuses to deal with it because she's too busy planning the next birthday party."

It was clear that I was now a member of an extremely conflicted team in desperate need of leadership. Believe it or not, I actually missed Dr. Right. He may not have won any popularity contests, but he could make tough decisions, and they were usually the right ones. Plus, he wasn't afraid of conflict. Although Glinda was better at opening lines of communication than Dr. Right was, she clogged the pipeline with propaganda rather than purpose or progress.

The next day, I met with Glinda to discuss an idea. I knew we had to get smarter with expenses, and I didn't want to see more people get laid off. I had been studying our health-care benefits over the past few weeks and noticed that they were very generous compared to what other companies offered. I suggested that we lower some of the benefits to save money, at least until we got sales back on track. Again in this meeting, I witnessed how Glinda backed away from conflict and avoided the tough issues. Knowing that a decision like this would not be popular, she refused to even discuss it.

Yet she must have discussed it with Shelly because, that night, I got this e-mail:

> To: Mike, VP of Finance
> From: Shelly, VP of Human Resources
>
> Re: Benefits Reduction
>
> Mike,
>
> I understand that you suggested a reduction in health-care benefits as a cost saving measure. I want to let

you know that I spent months creating the new benefits package that we just implemented a few months ago. Are you trying to make me look bad? Benefits are a human resources issue, and that's my job. I'd appreciate it if you'd stick to finance.

Shelly

I could not believe what I'd just read. Our senior management team was working at cross-purposes with one another when we should be working together, and Glinda was not helping. Unbelievable! I wanted to throw the computer across the room.

To the outside world, it looked as if we were one big happy family, but in reality, it was a façade. Although the parties, newsletters, coffee hours, and Employee of the Month awards were well intentioned, they were simply diversions from the truth about what was really going on. Things were going to have to change if we were going to survive. I wanted to help bring about that change…but how?

A MIDNIGHT MESSENGER

Thankfully, I was distracted from Shelly's e-mail by the sound of footsteps outside my office. It was Marty from the mailroom.

"Mike! It's good to see you," Marty said. "How's life treating you?"

"Aw, Marty, you don't want to know. I just uncovered a hornet's nest in here, and I don't know what to do about it."

Marty pulled up a chair. "I'm here if you just want to vent."

"Here, read it and weep."

I showed Shelly's message to Marty.

"Ouch," he said, shaking his head. "Looks like you've stepped on Shelly's toes. What do you intend to do about it?"

"What do I intend to do about it? Nothing! This is Glinda's problem, not mine."

"Are you sure you don't have a problem? Because that vein popping out on your forehead says otherwise. I think you *do* have a problem. So tell me, **what's the most difficult or important issue you have to deal with right now?**"

"Our leadership team is imploding, Marty. Even though it's going to tick somebody off, Glinda needs to step up and take control of the situation now. She has to deal with this conflict and make some tough decisions."

"Do you think she'll do that?" asked Marty.

I thought for a few minutes and replied, "Probably not. Look, don't get me wrong. Glinda has a lot of great qualities. I'll even jot some of them down, just as I did when we were talking about approaching Dr. Right." I grabbed a pad of paper and wrote:

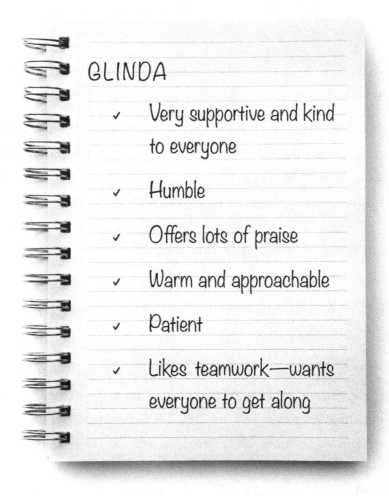

"That's it!" I said. "Glinda just wants us all to get along. To her, relationships trump all. She believes if she makes a tough decision, one or more members of her team are going to be disappointed. She would never want to take any action that would make someone unhappy, even if it were in our best interest for her to do so. I don't know if she even sees how unstable we really are!"

"But Marty," I continued, "with Glinda's leadership style, it would be extremely difficult, if not impossible, for her to confront and resolve this conflict we've got brewing on our team. It's just not in her wheelhouse, period."

"So," Marty interrupted. "Let me ask you again. **What's the most difficult or important issue you have to deal with right now?**"

I thought for a minute. "Our leadership team is a mess. We're not communicating with one another in a respectful, productive way. Consequently, we're not nearly as effective as we could be, and Glinda seems powerless to intervene. So if I want things to change, I have to find a way to resolve this directly with my peers so that we can show Glinda a unified recommendation."

"Good thinking. Sounds like you've had a breakthrough, Mike," Marty said. **"So why would your peers want to talk to you?"**

"Right now, I'm not so sure they *would* want to talk to me, especially Shelly. But I believe that we all have some good ideas for solving these problems. In hindsight, I didn't think. I overstepped my bounds by sharing ideas about benefits with Glinda before making sure I was on the same page as Shelly. If the problem is our inability to increase sales and retain customers, I should be offering to help Renaldo to come up with ideas. In fact, I think we all want to achieve more and see this business grow, not to mention our careers. And it wouldn't hurt if we could figure out how to manage Glinda better too."

"It sounds as if the challenge comes in making yourself heard among your peers. **How can you speak their language so that your voice is heard?**"

I remembered Marty asking me that same question back when I was trying to figure out how to approach Dr. Right. The answer was in thinking about others' needs and priorities.

"Marty, if we're going to be a collaborative team, we have to start by listening to one another. We need to make sure that everyone's voice is heard. People don't want to be kept in the dark, and they don't like surprises. They want to be included in the problem-solving process. They have ideas, opinions, and perspectives, and they deserve the time to share them. I think I need to get my peers together to hash this out. Maybe if I ask good questions, we can come up with good ideas. But I don't know…I'm brand new in this VP position. Will the other leadership team members take me seriously? What if they tell me to get lost?"

"Don't you think that's a chance worth taking?" Marty asked. "Honestly now, **what have you got to lose?**"

Marty was right. Building collaborative relationships with my peers was worth the risk. Our company's welfare was at stake, and I was not going to let us go down without a fight. It was time for me to man up.

I immediately e-mailed my fellow department heads, inviting them to join me in the conference room first thing in the morning so we could sit down together and come up with some ideas for resolving our issues once and for all. I was so intent on writing the e-mail that I didn't even hear Marty leave.

BUILDING COMMITMENT

To my surprise, they all showed up for the meeting. Clearly, they wanted to resolve the problem as much as I did. Still, we needed some sort of structure so the conversation wouldn't become a free-for-all. I initiated things even though I had never done anything this bold before.

"First, I'd like to thank all of you for joining me this morning. It's obvious that we are beginning to lose sales to Gulfstream, and I believe we can all agree that's a problem that we must address."

"Darn right," Renaldo stated.

"I also believe we can all agree that there are many reasons why this is happening, and we each have ideas for solving the problem. But first, I have an apology to make. Shelly, I'm sorry for overstepping my bounds and suggesting that we cut benefits without talking it over with you first. You are correct. That's your area of responsibility and expertise, and I need to respect that."

"It's okay," Shelly chimed in. "I know you're just trying to help. I'm sorry if my e-mail sounded rude."

"No problem," I said. "I know you're just as frustrated as I am. I also have a sense that we're all frustrated with Glinda for not making some of the tough calls. It seems to me like she is trying to protect all of us and keep us together as one big happy family. But that will only work if we're open with one another. So today I thought we could discuss our ideas openly and then present our recommendation to Glinda as a team. If she sees that we're all aligned, I believe she'll support our recommendation."

"What have we got to lose?" asked Gina.

Hmmm, I thought, *that question sounds vaguely familiar!*

"Then let's get to it," I said.

I thought I'd use problem-solving questions. "I'd like to start by asking you a question: **What do we do well?** Why do customers like doing business with us?"

Renaldo jumped in with both feet. "Customers really appreciate that our sales team has been in place for over five years. My folks have great relationships with customers because they take the time to understand our customers' businesses."

"I think they also value the expertise of our engineering team," I added, nodding toward Gina, our VP of engineering. "Quality and on-time delivery have always been our top priorities, and some of the changes Gina's team has implemented in the past have made us industry leaders in that area."

Gina looked shocked that someone actually complimented her and her team.

Starting the dialogue with what we did well really got the group going on a positive note. It was obvious that there was a lot of pride in the room, but we'd never taken the time to celebrate our successes. I summed up everyone's comments and then moved on to my next question.

"If our goal is to retain customers, and better yet, attract new ones, **what do we need to do better, differently, or more often?**"

Renaldo again took the lead. "That's a great question, Mike. Our customers' biggest frustration is the amount of time it takes to get a quote from us. By the time they get an estimate from us,

Gulfstream is practically shipping product to them. Ideally, we should be able to turn most quotes around immediately, within 24 hours max."

"Good idea, Renaldo," Gina said.

Recognizing that we were on a roll, I continued. "Okay, we need to get quotes in the customers' hands immediately. **What is preventing that from happening today?**"

"I have an observation," Shelly said. "Renaldo, I see a lot of quotes sitting on your desk, waiting for approval. No offense, but can't someone else do that?"

"I wish," Renaldo replied. "I don't have the time or the desire to approve every quote. Like I said, my team has a lot of experience. They don't need me checking their work. But the hierarchy here is ridiculous. Some quotes are even being approved by Glinda. And my team has no flexibility with pricing when it comes to customization. We work off engineering's fixed-pricing schedule."

Gina jumped in. "That pricing schedule is really outdated, but I didn't realize that it mattered to you. Had I known this was a big problem, I would have looked at it a long time ago."

We continued to identify things that we could do better, differently, or more often, and I worked to keep us on track. Sure, there was some drama. There were a few arrows shot across the table, and not everyone agreed with some of the ideas. But I just kept the group moving by bring their attention back to my **Five Questions.** Our list of ideas quickly grew to six full pages of oversized flip chart paper.

"I believe we're all onto something here," I said. "It sounds like we agree on more things than we thought we would, and we have a lot of ideas for improvement. But we've all seen this happen before: teams that are long on ideas and short on execution. **So if you had to pick just one idea for implementation, what would it be?**"

Renaldo spoke up. (I was beginning to see a pattern here.) "Eliminate the hierarchy in the quote-approval process," he said.

"I agree with that," Shelly said.

"We have to update engineering's pricing guidelines," said Gina.

"I agree," I said.

In order to keep us moving forward with some specific actions, I then asked, "Okay guys, **how can each of you help?**"

As I anticipated, Renaldo went first.

"To eliminate the hierarchy in the quote approval process, I could generate some guidelines for my team to follow. That way they'd have the freedom to make more decisions on their own."

"It would be giving them freedom within a framework," Shelly added. "That framework should put Glinda's mind at ease, at least for the smaller deals. You and Glinda could just approve the largest deals."

"Exactly," Renaldo agreed.

"Mike, could you work with me to revise engineering's pricing guidelines?" asked Gina.

"Absolutely," I said.

To ensure that we'd all leave the meeting with a complete understanding of what had just occurred, I then asked the four **Agreement-Building Questions** I recalled from my dream workplace:

- What did we decide today?

- Who is going to do what? By when?

- Who needs to know about this?

- What is the message and the tone of that message?

We all agreed to take 48 hours to get our parts of the plan together. That would be just in time to present our ideas to Glinda at our weekly senior leadership team meeting.

Before we left, Shelly said, "Once Glinda hears these ideas we've come up with today, I think she'll see a simple and safe way to regain our competitive edge over Gulfstream. And Mike, our benefits are due to renew in a couple months. Let's work together to see if we can shave off some of the costs."

"Sounds great," I said.

"Or better yet," Renaldo interjected, "let's blow the lid off our sales goals so we can all reap the benefits!"

After just two hours, we left the room sharing high fives and fist bumps. I sensed that had never happened before, not even at an expensive ropes course or "trust fall" retreat.

I can't say our conversation with Glinda at the leadership team meeting went perfectly. She was glad to see that we all agreed about the improvements in engineering's pricing structure, but she was really nervous about our "freedom within a framework" approach to allowing the sales team to send customer quotes without management approval. It took a while, but we got her to agree to a 90-day pilot.

After that, whenever we had a problem to solve, we went back to those same **Five Questions** I'd used to build commitment to the solution for our Gulfstream problem:

- What are we doing well?

- What could we do better, differently, or more of?

- What's preventing those improvements right now?

- If you could only pick one improvement, what would it be?

- How can you help?

These questions led to some pretty deep thinking and some lengthy conversations. In fact, I wasn't the only one working late anymore. My peers and I often got totally wrapped up in our dialogue as we worked toward building commitment around our ideas and goals. Even our meetings were a lot more energizing because we actually talked about tougher issues and generally reached agreements everyone could feel committed to.

Six months later, we were at one of Glinda's senior leadership team retreats. She was beaming with joy when she reported that our customer retention had increased for the first time in eight months and our sales were on target for the year. She also shared how happy she was that we were all working so well together. And she was right. We still had our disagreements; in fact, we had quite a few. After all, our leadership team was a diverse group of people with different backgrounds, experiences, and work styles. At least, now the disagreements were more fun.

But we were all caught off guard when Glinda made an announcement at the end of the meeting.

"I have been so blessed to work with this amazing team," she said, her eyes filling with tears and her voice shaking. "You've made my job here at Lakeside so easy, especially over the last few months. In fact, you've made these past few years of my career the best years of my life. But I have decided to retire to the beach. My husband has been retired for six years now, and it's time for me to join him."

"I'm going to miss you all so much," Glinda continued, doing her best to pull herself together. "But I'm comforted by the knowledge that I'm leaving you in very capable hands. You're going to love your new general manager. His name is Jack Leaper, and he starts on Monday."

CHAPTER 4

Chaos Abounds— The Open Workplace

We have nothing to hide.

Glinda's replacement, Jack Leaper, was no surprise to anyone. Jack was a former college football standout and graduate of the parent company's management development program—a real superstar on the sales side. He had earned a reputation throughout the company as a charismatic high achiever and also as being somewhat flamboyant. Honestly, I couldn't wait to meet him. After slogging through the last couple of years, all of us at Lakeside had every reason to believe that Jack Leaper had what it would take to whip our organization into shape.

I will never forget the day Jack arrived. He pulled up in a black SUV with a personalized license plate that read "VIPJACK." Standing 6' 5" and wearing a plush cashmere overcoat and gold cuff links, Jack, with his chiseled features and perfectly styled hair, looked like a cover model for GQ magazine. He certainly knew how to make a grand entrance. Crackling with energy, he burst through the door of our office suite and strode to the middle of the room, pausing for a moment to survey his new kingdom.

"Good morning, everyone! May I have your attention, please?" he called out. Puzzled faces began popping up one by one over the cubicle partitions.

"I am Jack Leaper, and I am delighted to be here. This is a historic day for all of us. Today everything changes for the better in this facility. We're going to make a difference for our customers. We're going to annihilate our competition. We're going to make this company a ton of money. And we're going to have a lot of fun while we're doing it. So buckle up everybody, because we're now on the fast track to greatness. VPs, meet me in my office in five minutes, please."

And in a swirl of cashmere and a cloud of cologne, he was gone.

Everyone stood frozen for a moment. Renaldo was the first to find his voice.

"What the—?" he said.

"Wow," said Shelly, her eyes wide.

"O. M. Geeeee!" Gina squealed, fanning her face and cracking us up.

"Well, you heard the man," I chuckled. "Let's 'buckle up for greatness' and go meet our new GM."

MR. LEAPER, TEAR DOWN THESE WALLS!

Initially I was intimidated by Jack's stature and his aggressive style, which I thought bordered on narcissism. But it didn't take long to see that he was sincere about his pledge to make our facility the best it could be, and he wasn't afraid to make big changes to do it. Those changes began on his first day in that initial meeting with Gina, Shelly, Renaldo, and me.

"As the former quarterback of a championship football team, I know a thing or two about how to inspire teamwork," he told us. "One of my many strengths is bringing my people together. So my first order of business is getting rid of those terrible partitions out there. From now on, this is a cubicle-free zone. Our people are not cattle; they don't belong in corrals. Let's open this place up so they can see and talk to one another."

And that was only the start. Within 30 days, Lakeside was practically unrecognizable. It used to be a place where everybody below the rank of senior manager was kept in the dark about the company's situation; now it was all about inclusion and information sharing. Jack installed the latest-model screens throughout the facility to broadcast news about our products, customers, competitors, and industry trends. He held the first of his monthly senior meetings where we spoke openly about new problems and new ideas. To help us solve problems and make decisions, Jack created several task forces and cross-functional groups that met on a weekly basis until the problems were solved or new ideas were implemented.

At Jack's Lakeside, people at all levels were free to talk about the good, the bad, and the ugly, something that had never happened under Glinda or Dr. Right. But probably the biggest change at Lakeside had to do with how conflicts and problems were managed. Jack actually *encouraged* confrontation and open disagreement, even if it might become heated.

"The quarterback can't win the game all by himself, no matter how great he is," he often said. "I want everyone on this team to be heard. You never know who's going to come up with the next game-winning play. Plus, I expect you to do a lot of blocking and tackling if someone threatens your position. We play to win."

Consequently, employee involvement across the company was at an all-time high. Information was plentiful and communicated through various channels. Our calendars were overflowing with meetings. Energy and activity levels were through the roof. But this was not just a bunch of feel-good busy work. Jack's management approach was actually having a positive impact on the bottom line. The company quickly made its short-term financial goals, and some of the expense cuts we had to implement during Glinda's tenure were rolled back. We were bringing in new people so quickly we didn't have time to train them all. They were given a list of essential competencies for their jobs and a host of classes and e-learning programs they could use on their own to build their skills. Otherwise, it was baptism by fire.

As for Jack, he was having the time of his life. His college football days were far behind him, but he was in charge of a winning team once more. He bounced from meeting to meeting to "huddle up" with managers and staff across functions. At his direction, his administrative assistant and the marketing department worked nonstop to submit nominations for Lakeside—and especially for *him*—to win awards, such as inclusion in the regional business journal's "Ones to Watch" edition and the 40 Under 40 honors. The trophy case he installed in his office began to sag under the weight of all the prizes he was winning. He seemed to love—no, crave—the attention.

And as for me and my peers…well, we spent our days and nights trying to keep our heads above water, wondering what brilliant new idea or activity Jack would come up with next. For the better part of a year, we worked 12-hour days. His energy was admirable, but his impulsiveness started to wear on us.

- Each senior team meeting resulted in the abrupt abandonment of our current projects and the hasty adoption of new ones. Consequently, things were starting to fall through the cracks, and we were losing direction.

- Jack's constant stirring of conflict made our workplace a lot like the weather in Buffalo: one minute a blizzard, the next minute a sunny day. Nobody knew what to expect.

- There were so many people involved in decision making that no decisions were actually being made. Consequently, good ideas languished, and some problems were not dealt with swiftly enough.

○ People were working harder than ever before, but they weren't working smarter. They reminded me of the Tasmanian devil from the cartoons I watched when I was young, spinning uncontrollably from one activity to the next. But we were never really moving forward.

Although people were more involved than ever, I don't think anyone really felt good about coming to work. Jack's fire hose approach to running an open workplace was a recipe for burnout, and people were dropping like flies. I had to admit, one of the best things about Glinda had been her ability to sense when someone was feeling stressed out. She really wanted people to feel good about what they were doing. But Jack? Either he couldn't see that people were in trouble, or he didn't care.

Things were going to have to change if we were going to survive this chaos. I wanted to help Jack bring about that change… but how do you convince the star quarterback that he's losing yardage when he's certain he's on the way to yet another blowout victory?

A VISIT FROM MESSENGER MARTY

I was at the office late one night, processing paperwork, when in walked Marty from the mailroom, making his rounds.

"Hey, Mike!" he said. "How's it going this evening?"

"Hi, Marty," I said with a sigh. "You know, it seems like every time I run into you, I've got some kind of sob story. Tonight's no exception."

Marty pulled up a chair. "Tell me about the problem."

"Another good person on my team just announced that he's leaving. Tanner is his name, and he gave the same reason as everybody else who's quit lately: he's tired of trying to keep up with Jack's ever-changing demands. I feel awful about losing Tanner, Marty. He's really bright, but he felt like no one appreciated that he had a life outside work. We waste too much time fighting fires, doing rework, and chasing down blind alleys. I don't blame him for wanting to find a better workplace."

"But Tanner's only the tip of the iceberg," I continued. "So many people here feel the same way. They can't take the chaos. But they can't find other jobs. So it's as if they've quit without leaving. They're just going through the motions. The pace Jack has set is exhausting, the priorities are always changing, and nobody knows what to expect next. We are finally starting to make a little progress around here, but at what cost?"

Marty didn't say a word. He just folded his arms and raised his eyebrows.

"I know, I know what you're about to ask," I said. **"What's the most difficult or important issue I have to deal with right now?"**

Marty nodded.

I thought for a minute and went on. "The lack of clarity, no doubt about it. Without clarity, we can't find the goal posts, and that's incredibly frustrating and tiring. Most people here mistake activity for results. They need to know where to focus their attention, collectively and individually. If only I could talk to Jack and convince him of this, we could turn things around."

"And why would he want to talk to you?"

"Because I have an idea for getting our team focused while simultaneously maintaining the momentum Jack's established, that's why."

"That sounds like something he would be interested in hearing. **How do you speak his language so that your voice is heard?"**

"These are the same questions you asked me back when I was trying to figure out how to approach Dr. Right and Glinda."

"I know. Consistency is my middle name. So let me ask you again: how do you speak Jack's language?"

"I have to figure out what's important to him so I can use those words when I speak with him."

"Excellent. You know what to do next."

"Yes, sir, I do!"

I got out a sheet of paper and a pen so I could make a list of all the things I knew for sure about Jack, and I reminded myself that to change the world, I have to change my thinking.

Here's what I wrote:

JACK:

- ✓ Has lots of energy, optimism, and enthusiasm

- ✓ Big picture, strategic thinker and loves new ideas

- ✓ Relationship-oriented

- ✓ Loves to be involved

- ✓ Wants to look good and be recognized

I reviewed my list and thought about what it meant. As I reflected on the times I'd seen Jack in action, I realized that his greatest fears were not being heard as well as anything that would damage his winning reputation. He wanted to include and be included. He felt that details and processes slowed him down, so he preferred to shoot first and ask questions later, leaving his team off balance.

"Since Jack will do anything to avoid being rejected or ignored, and since he values new ideas and big picture thinking so much, I'll have to appeal to those specific qualities when I approach him with my ideas," I said. "That's how I'll speak his language and prove to him that I respect his strategic mind and I care about winning as much as he does. That's the way to earn his confidence. But what if he sees my suggestions as a threat to his leadership?"

"Sounds to me like Jack always wants to be the most influential guy in the room," Marty replied, "so perhaps you can find a subtle way to find common ground with him. Make it clear that you are interested in *his* ideas. Let him know that your thoughts and suggestions are influenced by what you've learned from him. Make sense?"

"Sure does. He's more likely to take action if it's his idea. But in all honesty, he intimidates me, Marty. His big ego makes him menacing. I don't know about this …"

"Big thinkers always trump big egos, Mike. Don't you think it's worth taking a chance? **Honestly now, what have you got to lose?**"

"Nothing but frustration. This team is not going to achieve more if we don't make some changes soon. You know what? I'm on it, Marty," I said with resolve. "I'm going to talk to Jack."

"Good for you," Marty said. "I'll let you start putting together your game plan for approaching Jack. Good luck!"

"Thanks again, Marty," I said. As I watched him walk away, whistling, I wondered how that guy got to be so smart.

JACK, THE IDEA MAN

The next morning I paid Jack a visit in his office. I found him kicked back with his feet up on his desk, talking on the phone with someone I assumed was one of his former college teammates. They were arranging to meet up the following month to attend their alma mater's annual homecoming game. What perfect timing for the conversation I intended to have with Jack!

"I can't wait to see you guys again, Mario," Jack bellowed into the phone. "We're gonna have one helluva time, man." He spotted me standing in the doorway and energetically motioned for me to come in. I entered and walked over to look at his trophy case while he wrapped up his call.

"Listen, Mario, I have to let you go. We'll firm up our plans next week. Until then, don't do anything I wouldn't enjoy! Ha! Okay, brother, take it easy. Ciao!"

He hung up the phone, swung his size 14 feet to the floor, and walked over to stand beside me at the trophy case.

"What a team," he said pointing to a photo. "Division Two champs. Who knows what might have happened if I hadn't blown out my knee the summer before my senior year?"

"You probably wouldn't be at Lakeside right now. I'm not saying I'm happy that your playing career ended so early, but I *am* happy you're here. Things are much better since you took over."

"Thanks, Mike," Jack said. "I do my best."

"I know. Nobody works harder around here than you. We really appreciate your dedication and your ideas, Jack. And that's why I wanted to see you today. I'd like to get your ideas about something."

Jack slapped me on the back, practically knocking the wind out of me. "You came to the right place. Have a seat and tell me what you're thinking."

"Well," I said as we settled into the rich leather armchairs beside the trophy case, "we've lost some really good people over the past few weeks, and I worry that we might lose even more. In their exit interviews, they tell Shelly they're quitting because of a lack of direction."

"Aw, that makes no sense. We have a lot of great projects underway."

"You're right. We do have a lot of great opportunities. So it seems as if there's a disconnect between what *our people* think and what we think. For some reason we're not on the same page."

I motioned toward the trophy case. "Back when you were leading those championship football teams, how did you get all the different players to be on the same page?"

"That's easy. We put together a playbook at the beginning of the year and everybody had to learn it."

"What was in the playbook?"

Jack laughed. "You never played football, did you Mike? That's okay, pal. It's not for everybody. A playbook has individual plays in it that show each player what he has to do in order to either move his team forward or block the other team's progress."

"Sounds complicated."

I didn't bother mentioning my crew team experience. Now was not the time to drift off topic. This was all about focus.

"No, it's very simple. Depending on the position you play, you're instructed to either run this way, block this guy, or tackle that one. That's about it."

"But what about the team's goals? Aren't they in the playbook?"

"There's only one goal, and that is to win the championship."

"So everybody knows what game they're playing. They know what the championship is, and the playbook shows them exactly what they have to do to help the team win."

Jack nodded.

"Maybe if we had something like that at Lakeside, we wouldn't be losing so many good people."

Jack leaped to his feet and clapped his enormous quarterback hands together.

"Mike!" he shouted, "I have an idea. We're going to make a playbook for Lakeside!"

"Yes!" I said as I leaped to my feet. "Jack, you always have the best ideas."

"That's why they pay me the big bucks, my friend. That's why they pay me the big bucks. High five!"

And that's when our breakthrough occurred. I was able to speak Jack's language to get him to hear my voice and have confidence in me. He and I put together a team to create *The Lakeside Playbook* and roll it out facility-wide. The Playbook, only one page long, was intentionally simple and usable by everyone. It was built around the answers to these five questions:

1. What game do we play?

2. What championship are we trying to win?

3. What must be achieved in order to win the championship?

4. How will we keep score?

5. What differentiates us from other teams?

We all came up with a short and simple way to express our organization's purpose in the form of what game we played, and we had a clear vision to explain the championship we were all trying to win. To get to the championship, Jack created a set of overarching and measurable goals that he called the "big three." These same three goals applied to every team member in every department. To allow for new ideas, the "big three" was established for three-month periods. In other words, what did we need to achieve over the next three months in order to get to our championship?

As VP of finance and someone who loves reporting, I was tasked with turning the big screens into scoreboards. I had team members from across the organization identify what was important to measure, day in and day out, and this information was updated daily. That way, we knew whether we were on target in real time. And if we saw that we weren't, we could self-correct before too much damage was done. People began watching the scoreboards every day, and they really kept us focused.

Jack also had a great idea to answer that fifth question: What differentiates us from other teams? He scrapped Glinda's six values, which were too lengthy and confusing. Instead, he insisted that we emphasize the corporate Three Rs: respect, responsibility and results. He thought we'd look good in the eyes of the big wigs if we used the corporate values to guide our decision making and interactions with our team members, customers, and vendors. I'm not sure if I agreed with his rationale, but I knew that these core values would create clarity of expectations.

Thanks to the Playbook, the Three Rs, and the "big three," as well as our scoreboards, it wasn't long before every person working at Lakeside, from the newest team member to our seasoned veterans, knew what game we were playing, what championship we were trying to win, how we were keeping score, and how each one of us contributed to the effort. We finally had more clarity and commitment to a set of common goals throughout every department.

And whenever Jack was tempted to "call an audible at the line of scrimmage" and change our goals on the fly, we gently reminded him of his Playbook and our collective focus. Since we were speaking his language, he was able to rein himself in—usually with good humor too—and stick to the game plan.

The outcome was that Lakeside's financial results continued to grow. We exceeded our customer retention targets thanks to a significant improvement in on-time delivery, which we achieved while simultaneously cutting manufacturing costs and increasing efficiency. Fewer employees were calling in sick, and turnover was at its lowest in three years.

And even though we all knew Jack's star had to be rising, it wasn't until we received a visit from our parent company's CEO that we grasped the full extent of it.

CHAPTER 5

Patience and Hard Work Pay Off— The Collaborative Workplace

The more people know, the more
they can contribute.

W hen we received word that our CEO, Charlene E. Oppenhouse, would be coming to Lakeside for a visit, Jack swung into high gear. He wanted to make sure the plant was in tip-top shape and all of us were primed to impress. Actually, it wasn't hard to do. Although Jack's impulsiveness and high energy level still created havoc and sometimes wore people out, our systems and departments were running fairly well thanks to the Playbook, our "big three" goals, and the Three Rs. The Lakeside team was looking good.

Still, I wanted to be as prepared as possible from a personal standpoint, so as soon as I heard Charlene was flying in, I asked Jack to tell me about her.

"You'll like Charlene," Jack said. "She's very honest and direct, just like you: confident, results driven, focused. She expects a lot from the people around her, but she also expects a lot from herself. She wouldn't ask anything from us that she herself wouldn't do. She loves to compete, and she hates to lose. Come to think of it, Charlene would have been a great football coach."

"She sounds like an impressive person," I said.

"She is, but some people find her intimidating. She pulls no punches, I can promise you that. Her honesty can seem downright blunt sometimes, and she can't stand it if she thinks somebody is wasting her time."

From Jack's description, Charlene sounded like someone with strong dominant characteristics. I decided that if I had the opportunity to talk to her, one-on-one, I'd rely on the lessons I'd learned from Marty from the mailroom. If I want to achieve more, I have to think differently. Rather than just giving Charlene a laundry list of our various problems, I'd tell her about the most difficult or important issue we're dealing with right now. I thought about our current difficulties. First of all, we had a lot of people involved in all aspects of our operations, but we needed to be clearer about their individual roles and responsibilities. We weren't being proactive and deliberate about preventing problems, so we were still putting out fires as they occurred. We weren't being strategic about capitalizing on opportunities, either. We were simply jumping on interesting prospects but not following through on many of them because something shiny and new always came along to distract us.

And while it's true that people had been learning a lot, it wasn't always what they wanted to learn to help them grow in their careers. Jack's open workplace was full of engagement, but it was also full of chaos and burnout. We'd developed more focus and tools than we used to have. But we still didn't have the discipline to consistently apply those tools to have the right conversations, build commitment, make decisions, and drive results. And although people respected each other's expertise a lot more than in the past, they weren't confident that they could really trust each other.

These problems were evidence that we continued to suffer from a lack of true collaboration. So in a nutshell, that's how I would describe our most difficult issue to our CEO if I had the opportunity.

But why would our CEO want to talk to me about this issue? Because I have a solution. Jack said Charlene was bottom-line focused, so I'd focus on our biggest issue, lack of collaboration, and offer some proven ways to increase efficiency, save money, and drive profits. She'd also want to talk to me because I have a proven track record for getting the rest of the management team to solve problems collaboratively.

To make sure my voice was heard, I'd make an effort to **speak her language**. If Charlene is very direct, I wouldn't beat around the bush. I'd get straight to the point about how a more collaborative structure would drive the results she was looking for. I wouldn't take it personally if she seemed forceful or blunt. And I wouldn't be afraid to speak up.

At this point, I thought, **what have I got to lose?**

A MAJOR SHAKE-UP

My first look at Charlene E. Oppenhouse confirmed that she was, indeed, a no-nonsense woman. Wearing a classic dark blue suit and sensible shoes, and with her slightly graying hair pulled back in a neat bun, Charlene was the model executive. I'd have described her as a "steak and potatoes" kind of person: all business, zero fluff.

The first thing on Charlene's agenda was a town hall meeting with all the employees at which she announced that because of our successful completion of four key projects, Lakeside was now positioned to be the parent company's top choice for significant new business.

"Your teamwork and dedication have paid off," she said, "and I speak for the entire executive team in extending a sincere thank you and a hearty congratulations to each and every one of you, most notably to you, Jack Leaper, for your skillful leadership over the past two years. You and your people have turned this facility around and made it the winner it is today. I commend your efforts."

We joined Charlene in a round of applause. Jack stood alongside her, grinning from ear to ear.

"But I'm not here today just to thank all of you," Charlene continued, addressing the group. "I'm also here to make an announcement about an important organizational change. Jack will be leaving Lakeside later this month because he has been tapped to run global sales. Your new general manager will be named by the end of the day."

We all gasped at this shocking news.

"Jack, would you like to say a few words?" Charlene asked.

Jack stepped to the microphone and waited for the buzz in the crowd to subside. When we were finally quiet, he cleared his throat and spoke.

"On my first day at Lakeside, I told you we were on the fast track to greatness. I just had no idea the track would be *this* fast," he said, his voice cracking with emotion. "Guys, I really don't know how to thank you. You've been a great team, the best I've ever had the pleasure of coaching. Your strong work ethic and tireless contributions have led me to this moment of immense personal success, and I will be forever grateful to you."

After the town hall meeting, we VPs went out to lunch. Of course, the conversation centered around Jack's upcoming departure and the arrival of a new GM.

"Now that the initial shock has worn off, I have to say that I have mixed emotions about Jack leaving," Renaldo said. "The guy's made some major improvements around here, and I like him on a personal level."

"But he wears me out!" Gina said. "It's like having a puppy in the house. You have to watch him constantly because you never know what kind of mess he's going to get into next."

"Yeah, for me it's bittersweet, Jack leaving," Shelly said. "I liked a lot of what he brought to the table, and I'll miss his fun-loving energy. But you're right, Gina. He's a handful. And from an HR standpoint, we lost a lot of great people who simply became burnt toast in the chaos. What do you think, Mike?"

"I'm sorry to see Jack go," I said. "People were more involved and engaged than ever before, but without any structure, things became so crazy that everything took too much time. The Playbook is a big help. But we aren't as effective, efficient, or productive as we could be. If we're going to achieve more, we need more structure and discipline to help us really collaborate. Whoever our next GM is, I hope he or she understands that."

SPEAKING CHARLENE'S LANGUAGE

After lunch, Charlene appeared, unannounced, in my doorway.

"Hello, Mike," she said, tapping on the open door. "Got a minute?"

"Of course! Please come in."

Charlene sat across from me. "First of all, I want to apologize for taking you and the other VPs by surprise with my announcement this morning. It's just that the executive team thought it would be best to deliver this news swiftly and with minimal lead up. We didn't want the rumor mill to become a distraction. We thought this would be the least disruptive way to handle it, sort of like ripping off a bandage."

"I understand. It's a great move for Jack and the company."

"I'm glad you agree. You know, I've come to value your opinion quite a bit over the years," she said.

"*Value my opinion?* But we've never met before today."

"True, but that doesn't mean I haven't heard of you and your contributions to Lakeside's success."

Charlene went on to explain that my name first came up back when Dr. Right was reassigned to international R&D. Apparently, he told her I worked diligently to improve the quality of our reporting and our ability to make decisions.

"If I recall correctly, Dr. Right had the utmost confidence in you because you were an analytical, logical thinker who always focused on accuracy," she said. "The next time I heard your name was from Glinda Nurturino, who sang your praises for rallying the troops to build commitment during a period of great internal conflict for Lakeside."

I couldn't believe what I was hearing.

"And of course there's Jack Leaper, who tells me you're the glue that holds this entire facility together. He credits you for some great ideas to create clarity and focus across the various departments."

"Mike, I know the past few years have not been easy for you and your team," Charlene continued. "You've worked for some interesting people. The type of work done here at Lakeside makes

this our best location for giving high-potential people in our organization the opportunity to test their leadership skills. I realize
that's made the work environment challenging. And somehow
you've managed to get great results year after year. I'd love to hear
your take on what's worked and what hasn't worked during your
time at Lakeside."

This was the opportunity I'd been waiting for!

"And I'd be happy to tell you," I said.

THREE INEFFECTIVE WORKPLACES

I began by telling Charlene about the environment under Dr.
Right. "Dr. Right was brilliant, and he really liked to analyze
information and think about decisions," I said. "Quality was his
top priority. But he didn't have many conversations with us, and
his less-than-open style kept people in the dark. This discouraged
them from doing their best and created some real hostility among
coworkers. It caused everyone to feel and be defensive. I guess I'd
call what we had a **Defensive Workplace**. Only the person in the
top chair could do all the thinking. The rest of us defended our
positions."

I got out a pencil and paper and made this drawing:

"In the Defensive Workplace, our mission, vision, and values were not defined or even considered, so nobody knew where to focus. Employees rarely met one-on-one with their supervisors. The management team knew only the people in their immediate areas and never met informally with employees. We had limited or no information about our products, customers, financial position, competitors, or industry. It was like trying to drive at night with no headlights."

"I see," Charlene said.

"Achievements were seldom recognized," I continued. "All problems were solved by Dr. Right with no input from the employees; we didn't dare offer opinions or suggestions. In fact, initiative was sometimes punished. People were discouraged from asking questions that didn't pertain to their jobs. And the formality was suffocating. Official communication was shared with employees in writing, and the little communication we did have was uneven. Disagreements and conflicts were ignored or suppressed. Mistakes resulted in finger pointing. As a result, there was zero trust between the employees and the management team."

"No wonder this facility missed its projections back then," Charlene said. "It was clear there was a problem with teamwork here, and that's why we brought in Glinda. We were certain she'd be able to bring people together."

"And in many ways, she *did*," I said. "Glinda's number-one goal was to have us feel that we were all in this together. She was a real team builder who worked hard to keep people happy. To the outside world, we looked like one big happy family. But inside there was a lot of dysfunction that no one was allowed to discuss. It's ironic. Glinda was very kind and accommodating, yet the result was that she ran a highly **Paternalistic Workplace** in which people felt disrespected and degraded."

"Meaning?"

I added some chairs to my drawing.

"There were too many layers of bureaucracy here. You really had to go up the food chain to get anything accomplished, even cost estimates for customers," I continued. "Glinda and the senior managers were like parents, and everyone else was treated like a child. Only employees in a need-to-know position were given information about our products, customers, financial position, competitors, and industry. It was as if Glinda wanted to protect us from anything that might be the least bit unpleasant. We were encouraged to ask questions but only about the positive things. Everything else was hidden from us. We had a mission, vision, and values, but only senior management discussed them. Other than a few people, nobody else knew what they were. And conflicts and disagreements were not allowed."

"But that's impossible. Every organization has conflict."

"That's true. And that's why the Paternalistic Workplace was such an uncomfortable place to be. When people are discouraged from acknowledging and dealing with their conflicts, dysfunction spreads like wildfire. Who could focus on getting good results when they were seething over a problem they weren't allowed to solve? It was all about maintaining harmony no matter what the cost."

Charlene nodded.

"In our Paternalistic Workplace, the interaction between people and their supervisors was a one-way street. Some employees met with their supervisors occasionally, but it was primarily to get instructions. Supervisors only explained things when it was an emergency or a rush priority. All other information was learned through the rumor mill. Employees might have trusted their immediate supervisors and coworkers, but they weren't so sure about senior management or the people in other departments. There was always a lot of politics, an undercurrent of suspicion and a feeling of oppression."

"No wonder Jack Leaper was able to make such amazing progress when he stepped in," Charlene mused.

"The difference was like night and day," I said. "From the moment Jack set foot in the building, we could tell he was determined to run an **Open Workplace** where people could brainstorm, get great results, lift one another up, even butt heads when they needed to."

"And from your perspective, how did it go?"

"Our results speak for themselves. We've made huge strides. We developed mission, vision, and values statements in the form of our Playbook and scoreboards. Everyone can explain our current goals and priorities. Employees regularly meet one-on-one with their supervisors and coworkers to share ideas and ask questions. In fact, Jack initiated an explosion of teams, tasks forces, and cross-functional groups to solve problems and make decisions."

I was on a roll now.

"There's a sense that management has nothing to hide, which is a big change from the past," I said. "Everyone knows about our products, top customers, financial position, competitors, and industry, particularly if the information impacts their jobs. There are plenty of training programs available for skill building too, which give people the opportunity to grow and rise in the ranks. We host regular meetings with employees to share both good and bad news, and all employees are encouraged to ask about anything and express their opinions freely. Disagreements are openly addressed, and achievements are recognized at various levels within the company."

"The Open Workplace sounds like a terrific place to be," Charlene said.

"It is…for a while." I drew another picture.

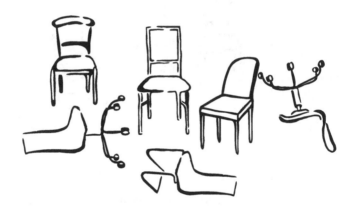

"Even though there's much more involvement than in the Defensive and Paternalistic Workplaces we had before, it is chaotic and stressful," I said. "We've lost a lot of great people to burnout. Their chairs just toppled over. Without a solid structure, the Open Workplace can become a runaway train."

"Sounds like we still have some room for improvement here at Lakeside," Charlene said. "Mike, if you could design the ideal workplace, what would it be like?"

"It would be what I call the **Collaborative Workplace.** I've been dreaming of it for years."

"Go on," Charlene said, leaning forward.

"The Collaborative Workplace is designed to foster structured collaboration to get the best results for the organization. In this environment, employees are able to explain how their work contributes to the mission and vision and how they demonstrate the company values every day. That's because they are briefed regularly on the organization's long-term goals, how they were determined, and how they influence current priorities."

"There's a lot of communication across the organization," I continued. "Every chair is different, because we are all respected for our unique perspectives, talents, and work styles. But we all act as if we're at the same level. Employees and their supervisors have frequent, mutually beneficial conversations. Senior managers host regular events and often walk around the facility to stay in touch. Sometimes you don't even recognize them because they treat everyone like peers. Intimidating titles don't have to exist, because they don't matter. People are free to make decisions about their work, and their decisions are usually spot on because they understand things such as what makes an ideal customer, as well as the company's products, financial position, competitors, and industry."

The more I explained the Collaborative Workplace, the more excited I became. From the pleased look on Charlene's face, I could see that even she was caught up in my vision of the ideal workplace. I pressed on.

"When new employees are brought in, they receive a thorough orientation so they understand not only their roles but also how they fit into the bigger organizational picture. They get ongoing coaching from senior managers and even their peers. Their individual development is based on their strengths and their personal career goals. Achievements are recognized and celebrated at every level. In fact, employees are rewarded for challenging the status quo and for being innovative. They actively practice problem prevention, but when the inevitable problem does crop up, it's solved collaboratively and in a structured way. Disagreements and conflicts are widely viewed as healthy and are used to improve the work environment. And all this results in employees and management having complete trust, even confidence, in one another. I believe the Collaborative Workplace is the only way to create a sustainable, competitive advantage for the Lakeside facility. I sure hope our new GM shares my dream."

"I do too, Mike," Charlene said. "I do too. But like most grand plans, it's probably much easier said than done."

"Oh it's definitely doable. I'm certain of it. I've got it all mapped out. There are a bunch of tools that we could use more consistently to have this breakthrough. They can be divided into what I call the five Cs: confidence, conversations, commitment, clarity, and courage. And they are really simple. I've been practicing them during my years here at Lakeside."

"Is that so? Well, how about this, Mike Learner. If you can tell me exactly how you'd implement these five Cs of yours, I will name you Lakeside's new general manager today."

Charlene stood and extended her hand.

"Do we have a deal?" she asked.

I could hardly believe this was happening.

"Yes ma'am, we do!" I said, shaking her hand.

"Terrific. Let's make a pot of coffee, and you can tell me all about it."

PART TWO

IDENTIFY YOUR WORKPLACE

Identify Your Workplace

Take this short quiz to identify which of the four workplaces exists in your organization. Start by selecting the response that best matches what you see or feel in your current workplace.

1. Statements explaining the organization's purpose, such as a mission or vision, as well as organizational values are:

    a.   Not defined or even considered.

    b.   Defined but only known by a few people.

    c.   Defined and known by many people.

    d.   Clearly defined and employees can explain how their work contributes to them.

2. When it comes to goals and priorities:

a. Senior managers might talk about them but employees do not know what they are.

b. Supervisors explain only emergency or rush priorities.

c. Supervisors and employees can explain short-term goals and priorities.

d. Employees are briefed regularly on long-term goals, how they were determined, and how they affect short-term priorities.

3. Senior managers:

a. Know only the people in their immediate areas and almost never meet with employees.

b. Occasionally present to employees in formal meetings.

c. Have nothing to hide. They host regular events to share both good and bad news.

d. Are connected with employees and often walk around to stay in touch.

4. Much of the information I get is:

a. In writing as official communication. Whatever communication exists is uneven.

b. From my supervisor or through the rumor mill.

c. Plentiful and sometimes overwhelming.

d. Organized in a way that the right information is easy to get.

5. Employees meet with their direct supervisor:

a. Rarely or only when concerns arise.

b. Once in a while, mainly to get instructions or to get problems solved.

c. Regularly, to share ideas and ask questions.

d. Frequently, and have mutually beneficial conversations.

6. When employees have opinions or ideas for improvement:

   a.   They do not share them. In fact, initiative may be punished.

   b.   They share them with their supervisors who decide how to proceed.

   c.   They are encouraged to share and discuss them with others.

   d.   They are rewarded for challenging the way we do things
        and encouraged to explore their ideas further.

7. Problems are solved:

   a.   By senior managers with little or no input from employees.

   b.   By direct supervisors who hear the bad news and take care of
        problems, as they strive to maintain harmony in their groups.

   c.   By many people who are encouraged to work on
        teams, task forces, and cross-functional groups.

   d.   By team members who work collaboratively, in
        structured ways to solve and prevent problems.

8. Disagreements or conflict are:

   a.   Ignored or suppressed.

   b.   Discouraged. Mistakes result in finger pointing.

   c.   Openly expressed. We talk about the
        good, the bad, and the ugly.

   d.   Viewed as healthy differences and used
        to improve our work environment.

9. Employees:

   a.   Have little authority to make decisions about their work.

   b.   Can make some decisions but have to
        check with their supervisors.

   c.   Have freedom to make decisions about their work, but few
        guidelines or support exist for making good decisions.

   d.   Have freedom to make decisions about their
        work based on established guidelines.

10. Professional development includes:

    a.   Mostly learning on-the-job as you go.

    b.   Some training programs to increase job skills.

    c.   Coaching from supervisors and training programs in a variety of areas.

    d.   Ongoing training, on-the-job experiences, and working with different people who help me achieve my professional and personal goals.

11. When it comes to trust:

    a.   Employees have little trust in management or co-workers. They don't feel trusted by others either.

    b.   Employees may trust their immediate supervisors and co-workers, but aren't so sure about other managers or departments.

    c.   Employees and managers respect one another's knowledge and skills.

    d.   We have an environment of trust. Team members at various levels have confidence in one another.

12. The organization's philosophy for sharing information with employees most closely sounds like:

    a.   The less said the better.

    b.   We only talk about the good things.

    c.   We have nothing to hide.

    d.   The more people know the more they can contribute.

Add Your Scores Here:

A's: _____ B's: _____ C's: _____ D's: _____

IF YOU HAVE MOSTLY A'S: You have a Defensive Workplace

It may seem hopeless right now as you most likely see elements of Lakeside Manufacturing's Defensive Workplace when Dr. Right made all the decisions. But know you have the power to create your dream workplace. It will take time and patience. Review your quiz responses and pick a safe and easy place to start. One small breakthrough at a time will help others have confidence in you as someone who can make changes while building relationships. One word of caution – don't try to jump from Defensive to Collaborative too quickly. Over time, you will see your organization becoming more Paternalistic and then more Open as you move toward a Collaborative Workplace. This is a normal transition as your coworkers become more comfortable with your new ways of operating and gain the courage to try them on their own.

IF YOU HAVE MOSTLY B'S: You have a Paternalistic Workplace

This is a very common workplace. Making progress will take effort, but you can do it! You may see many elements of Lakeside Manufacturing's hierarchical culture when Glinda Nurturino was General Manager. Although it might seem to the outside world like you're one big happy family, those on the inside see the problems. Review your quiz responses to identify your most important or difficult problem. Then, study the back of this book for breakthrough tools and diplomatic ways of driving change while keeping the peace.

IF YOU HAVE MOSTLY C'S: You have an Open Workplace

You're almost there! You may see many elements of Lakeside Manufacturing's chaotic culture when Jack Leaper was at the helm. You're informed, involved and, most likely, juggling a lot of balls every day. This can be energizing at times, while draining and stressful at others. Fine tuning your culture by implementing the ideas at the back of this book is an essential next step for your ongoing success.

IF YOU HAVE MOSTLY D'S: You have a Collaborative Workplace

Congratulations! You may see many elements of Mike Learner's dream workplace in your real life workplace. Study the survey questions to identify where you have opportunity to improve. The rest of this book will give you more ideas for building collaboration with your team. Note that sometimes all four workplaces exist within one organization. Think about how you can inspire other teams within your organization to increase their level of collaboration with others.

Your team can take the full Collaboration Breakthrough Employee Survey. Visit **www.CollaborationBreakthrough.com** for more information.

PART THREE

THE 5 C'S OF A COLLABORATIVE WORKPLACE

CHAPTER 5

Confidence

Confidence begins with me.

—*Mike Learner*

Confidence is a difficult thing to describe because it's not something you do, it's something you feel. And when you don't *feel* confident in your coworkers, it's impossible to get anything done. Without confidence, you can't be sure your teammates will deliver what they promise. You worry that your interests won't be represented in your absence. People don't seem to care about the work or, more importantly, each other. And if you share critical feedback with your coworkers, you can't be sure it won't be taken personally or defensively.

In the Collaborative Workplace, coworkers have complete confidence and trust in one another. But confidence doesn't come about by accident. The Collaborative Workplace is supported by tools to convey what's expected of everyone, and people from all levels of the organization use these tools to build trusting relationships. In fact, they go one step further. As Mike Learner does, they proactively look for ways to become more confident in one another. Without that confidence, essential functions such as communication, delegation, idea sharing, and consensus just don't happen.

FLASHBACK...

DR. RIGHT'S PERSPECTIVE

After spending most of my career in research and development, I accepted the position as Lakeside's general manager. I was eager to take this new position because I truly enjoyed working in a capacity where I had direct input on the product as well as a certain level of autonomy. But once I was in the GM role, I felt I couldn't count on anyone. I'd give people assignments, and I'd have to go back and fix their mistakes. My project managers wouldn't hold their teams accountable, and as a result, we were missing our on-time delivery targets and budget goals.

Science has made me a skeptic; therefore, from my perspective, critical feedback is one of the most important ingredients to success. Unfortunately, most of my direct reports are offended when I give them constructive criticism. I find managing people the most draining part of my job. I feel I have to do everything myself. I never really wanted to manage people, but it was the only way to get into a higher pay grade.

I was relieved when Mike Learner approached me with his ideas for fixing the *Cost of Goods Sold* report. The poor quality of that report had been bothering me for quite some time. Mike's a smart guy, and he cares about doing things right. He didn't even mind when I red-penned his first two drafts. He'll make a great GM.

CREATING CONFIDENCE

A Collaborative Workplace is only as strong as the relationships that exist between team members. The foundation of those relationships is confidence and trust.

There are five factors that drive confidence and trust among coworkers. They are:

Confidence Factors

1.   Competence: coworkers feel confident that others are good at what they do.

2.   Openness: coworkers feel confident that they can be honest and that others will be open to their ideas and input.

3.   Reliability: coworkers feel confident that others will deliver what they promise.

4.   Fairness: coworkers feel confident that they are treated fairly.

5.   Caring: coworkers feel confident that others care about what's important to them and consider their well-being before making decisions.

If one or more of these five factors is missing or damaged, it will break down people's confidence in their coworkers and make it very difficult, if not impossible, to collaborate effectively. Consider the first confidence factor, competence. If you believe a teammate lacks the necessary skills to do the job, you're not going to feel confident delegating a task to that person. Or consider the second confidence factor, openness. If you don't feel you can have an honest conversation with a team member, you're not likely to have confidence that you can confront tough issues and solve problems together. What about reliability? If a team member doesn't always follow through, how can you trust that person to meet an important deadline? When it comes to fairness, if you're not sure a teammate will behave even-handedly and operate in good faith, you'll always be watching your back. And finally, if team members don't seem to care, how can you be confident that they will always do their best to further the team's goals and objectives rather than just their own?

The good news is that you can assess and influence the presence of these five confidence factors in three ways: the confidence people have in you, the confidence you have in other individuals, and the confidence team members have in the group as a whole. The rest of this chapter will provide simple tools for assessing and improving all three.

BREAKTHROUGH TOOL: CONFIDENCE QUIZ

See How Confident People Are in You

Many times, when reading self-help books, we think about all the people we know who could really benefit from implementing the ideas. Yet we can't expect others to improve if we aren't willing to take the first step ourselves. That's why each of us has to start by looking in the mirror and asking, "Do people have confidence in me?"

Are you competent? Do you do your job well? Do you deliver what you promise? When someone comes to you wanting to have a tough discussion, how do you react? Are you open to constructive criticism and feedback, or are you defensive? Do you treat others fairly? Do you show them that you care about the things that are important to them?

Take the Confidence Quiz to understand your strengths and how you can build others' confidence in you.

Confidence Quiz

Take this quiz to see how easy it is for others to have confidence in you. Rate yourself on each statement using the following scale:

1 = almost never

2 = rarely

3 = sometimes

4 = often

5 = almost always

COMPETENCE	
	I have the knowledge, skills, and ability to do my job well.
	I do my job correctly and do not make mistakes.
OPENNESS	
	My teammates talk to me about everything, even the most difficult issues.
	I avoid coming across as critical, defensive, or disinterested when speaking with teammates.
RELIABILITY	
	I deliver what I promise.
	I show up on time and meet deadlines.
FAIRNESS	
	I stay impartial and objective in decision making, avoiding actions that might seem as if I play favorites.
	I reach out to include others to avoid gossiping or the appearance of hidden agendas.
CARING	
	I consider the well-being of my teammates before making decisions.
	I genuinely try to get to know what others care about, professionally and personally, so I can show that I care about those things too.
ADD YOUR SCORES HERE: _____	

ANALYZE YOUR SCORE:

40 or more: People most likely have a lot of confidence in you. Don't rest on your laurels, though. Confidence and trust can be lost very easily. Keep up the good work.

30–39: Some people may have confidence in you, while others may not. Identify which relationships need to be strengthened and take action to do so.

Less than 30: You have some work to do. Building others' confidence in you will take time. Start with one of the questions in the quiz. What actions can you take to enhance your score? Get started today!

BREAKTHROUGH TOOL: CONFIDENCE INVENTORY

See How Much Confidence You Have in Other People

A second area of focus is the amount of confidence you have in your peers, bosses, direct reports, and other coworkers. If you don't have confidence in them, are you open to taking steps to fix that? We certainly hope so, because if you're not confident in the people around you and you don't do anything to address it, it severely diminishes your role as a collaborative team member. Use the following Confidence Inventory to get started.

Take the Confidence Inventory

Write each of your teammates' names across the top row. Then, using the definitions of the five confidence factors, rate your teammates on how well they demonstrate each factor, using the following scale:

1 = almost never

2 = rarely

3 = sometimes

4 = often

5 = almost always

CONFIDENCE FACTORS	Teammate #1	Teammate #2	Teammate #3	Teammate #4	Teammate #5
COMPETENCE: He/she is good at his/her job.					
OPENNESS: I can have an open discussion with him/her.					
RELIABILITY: He/she delivers what is promised.					
FAIRNESS: He/she treats me fairly.					
CARING: He/she considers my well-being before making a decision.					
TOTAL:					

Put a checkmark next to areas of low confidence.

Do you spot any trends?

_____

_____

Is there one person with low scores across the board?
Use the ideas in the next sections to identify how you
can enhance your relationship with this person.

_____

_____

Is there one confidence factor that you rated consistently low
for everyone? Use the ideas in the next section to fix that.

_____

_____

- -

BREAKTHROUGH TOOL:
TEAM CONFIDENCE INVENTORY

See How Much Confidence Individuals Have in the Whole Team

A third area of focus is the amount of confidence team members
have in each other as a whole team. Without confidence, there is
no collaboration, so evaluating a team's level of trust in the whole
and addressing any shortcomings is an ongoing task.

Take the Team Confidence Inventory

Copy and distribute these questions to your team. Ask them to think about the team as a whole. Then, choose a rating for each of the five confidence factors using the following scale:

1 = almost never

2 = rarely

3 = sometimes

4 = often

5 = almost always

	MY TEAM AS A WHOLE
COMPETENCE: We are good at what we do.	
OPENNESS: We have open discussions without becoming defensive.	
RELIABILITY: We deliver what we promise to each other and the organization.	
FAIRNESS: We treat each other fairly.	
CARING: We consider the well-being of others before making decisions.	

Share results with your teammates to create a group score. What are the team's strengths? How can you capitalize on those strengths? What could the team do better, differently, or more often to improve in weak areas? Put a plan together to get started right away.

BREAKTHROUGH TOOL: CONFIDENCE BUSTERS

So you've taken the quiz and found that your confidence and trust could be improved. Start by determining if you're doing anything that breeds mistrust. Some common actions that cause people to lose confidence in a person or a team are listed below. Put a checkmark next to the Confidence Busters that are getting in the way of complete confidence.

☐ Unresolved personal conflict

☐ Restricted freedom

☐ Lack of control

☐ Inadequate support

☐ Closed or guarded communication

☐ Red tape and bureaucracy

☐ Lack of recognition

☐ Stealing credit

☐ Unwillingness to share expertise

☐ Low tolerance for ambiguity

☐ Obsession with details

☐ Desire to work alone vs. involve others

☐ Behind the scenes conversations

☐ Gossip

☐ Mandates and dictates

☐ Absence of ground rules

☐ Inflexible, inconsistent directions

☐ Abdicating responsibility/finger pointing

☐ Workplace secrets

☐ Poor measurement systems

☐ Inconsistent policies

What other Confidence Busters impact your team?

_____

_____

_____

_____

What steps can you take to eliminate these Confidence Busters?

_____

_____

_____

_____

BREAKTHROUGH TOOL: CONFIDENCE BUILDERS

Use the checklist below to identify ways to build others' confidence in you, your confidence in others, or the confidence among your team. They have been categorized by confidence factor so you can zero in on your trouble spots. Get started immediately to build confidence and create collaboration in your workplace.

COMPETENCE

- ☐ Competency and skill development
- ☐ Link individual efforts to the bigger picture
- ☐ Identify external threats and challenges
- ☐ Coaching and mentoring
- ☐ Praise and encouragement

OPENNESS

- ☐ Personal disclosure
- ☐ Willingness to be vulnerable
- ☐ Candid words and caring tone
- ☐ Honest communication

RELIABILITY

- ☐ Clear expectations
- ☐ Personal accountability
- ☐ Consistency, certainty, dependability
- ☐ Maintain confidentiality

FAIRNESS

- ☐ Fair, equitable, impartial treatment
- ☐ Cooperation
- ☐ Share resources

CARING

- ☐ Accept and value others' differences
- ☐ Freedom from harm/hurt
- ☐ Listen carefully
- ☐ Supportive relationships

What other ideas do you have that aren't listed above?

_____

_____

_____

What steps can you take to put these Confidence Builders into action?

_____

_____

_____

Most importantly, show your confidence in another person. By taking the first step, you can create the Collaborative Workplace you desire.

Takeaway Tips

- ○ Confidence is the foundation of every relationship and, therefore, every collaborative team.

- ○ Confidence occurs when teammates know they can fully believe in one another's level of competence, openness, reliability, fairness, and caring (the five confidence factors).

- ○ These five confidence factors can be assessed using the Confidence Quiz, Confidence Inventory, and Team Confidence Inventory.

- ○ Use the Confidence Builders and Confidence Busters to create your action plan.

CHAPTER 7

Conversations

What we have is not a failure to
communicate but a failure to converse.

—Mike Learner

I
f you were to ask your coworkers, "What's the number-one
improvement we could make to enhance our workplace?"
most often, the answer would be a unanimous vote for "better
communication." In fact, no one—including senior leadership—
is surprised when employee surveys reveal this fact. In response,
organizations create posters, mugs, pens, and T-shirts to profess
their philosophies, develop newsletters to share more information,
hold town hall meetings to deliver the annual "state of the union"
address, and send more and more e-mails.

These are all great ideas, especially for sharing and reinforcing information, and generally people feel more informed when these things are in place. But sometimes the information is inconsistent or conflicting, leaving people confused. At other times, the information is so plentiful it's as if it's being sprayed over the workforce from a fire hose, leaving people overwhelmed. These are tell-tale signs that an Open Workplace exists. People are involved and informed but overwhelmed and confused.

These communication vehicles also serve as public relations campaigns for senior management and the organization, so communication happens in a top-down or one-way direction rather than among coworkers. And despite these best efforts, employees still complain that communication is broken.

The crux of the matter is that when you ask people why *they* really think communication is poor in their organizations, they say it's because they can't speak openly with the person sitting next to them or down the hall. Their department doesn't communicate with other departments, so they're not working in tandem. And they're avoiding tough discussions. They're not having good collaborative conversations with one another.

Therefore, the problem cannot be summed up with the blanket statement "we have a communication problem." The truth of the matter is we're really searching for ways to have meaningful, productive, solutions-focused conversations with the people around us.

FLASHBACK...

GLINDA NURTURINO'S PERSPECTIVE

Corporate moved me to the position of general manager at Lakeside because morale at the plant was at an all-time low. I believe it's important for people to be happy in their work; it makes them feel much more productive and satisfied by the workplace. Relationships are the glue that holds the organization together. Sometimes it takes a long time for me to make decisions because I'm always looking for the win-win solution. I believe that harmony in the organization is imperative. When conflict arises, I typically let people work things out on their own, as Mike Learner and the team did when our client left us for Gulfstream. I'm so proud of Mike. He'll make a great GM. He believes the same things I do: that it's vital that team members understand how important they are to me and the organization as a whole.

CREATING CONVERSATIONS

There are three types of conversations that team members in a Collaborative Workplace must master:

o   Coaching Conversations are a tool for solving problems, generating ideas, and encouraging others to succeed.

o   Straight-Talk Conversations are a tool for bringing up a difficult problem or something that's bothering you with someone else.

o   Agreement-Building Conversations are a tool for building alignment and making sure that everyone is on the same page.

As you read more about these conversations, you'll see that they all use a questioning strategy rather than a telling strategy. *Telling* people what to do can be perceived as demanding and degrading, and it puts people on the defensive. *Asking questions* demonstrates humility, opens up dialogue, and encourages participation. These conversation tools are the secrets to improving communication and increasing collaboration in your workplace.

The good news is that it's possible to master all three of these essential conversations relatively quickly. The hardest part is getting started, which is why we developed a set of scripts to help you get the ball rolling. Once you get the conversation going by setting the right tone, things will go just fine.

- -

BREAKTHROUGH TOOL: THE COACHING CONVERSATION SCRIPT

In Collaborative Workplaces, Coaching Conversations happen every day. Let's take the most basic example. At work, especially when you're a manager, people might often come to you with their concerns, complaints, and problems. They expect you to solve problems for them because you're good at it. But if you don't respond with a good Coaching Conversation, you run the risk of becoming trapped in the troubleshooter role. Some managers even start to feel resentment when it seems that their team members have quit thinking for themselves. The flip side is the employee who, whenever he asks his manager for advice is simply told what to do and then dismissed to go do it. It's as if the manager is listening only with the intent to *reply* rather than the intent to understand. There's nothing collaborative about that.

Most of us don't want somebody else to solve our problems for us. We want the satisfaction of finding our own solutions. You can help your teammates feel that same sense of satisfaction by having Coaching Conversations with them.

A Coaching Conversation has three parts:

1. **Tell Me About.** Beginning a conversation with "Tell me about..." gets you off to a great start. First, it slows the conversation down so you both can clear your heads and think. It lets the other person know that he/she is important to you and that you want to listen. It's also your cue to avoid diving into problem-solving mode, while being a good listener and coach. Try starting a Coaching Conversation with:

    > `"Tell me about your concern."`

    or

    > `"Tell me about your idea."`

2. **What?** Once you ask the other person to tell you about the problem, the floodgates may open. After that person has laid it all out on the table, it's time to reel it in and keep the conversation proactive and solutions oriented. So ask a question that begins with what and is designed to set a goal. This shifts the conversation in a positive and proactive way. For example:

> What would you like to see happen?

or

> What are you trying to achieve?

or

> What, ultimately, would you
> like the outcome to be?

3. **How?** Once the outcome is determined, it's time to build a plan. So ask a question that begins with how and is designed to create a process or plan for action. For example:

> How can you make that happen?

or

> How can you achieve that goal?

or

> How can you get the resources
> you need to succeed?

Notice the use of the word you in these three examples rather than the word I. The purpose of a Coaching Conversation is to help someone learn, grow, and feel more confident. It isn't designed for the coach to take on more work. Initially, you might find that people struggle to identify their goals or to create action plans, especially if they are not used to having conversations like this. If this is the case, you can give them a couple of ideas or ask them to take some additional time to think about your questions.

If you consistently use these words, Tell me about ... (to really understand), What ...? (to set a goal), and How ...? (to create a plan), you'll see that team members are more prepared for discussions. And, don't forget to **celebrate successes,** highlighting specific actions and accomplishments. It's the easiest and most fun way to keep co-workers on track for the future.

One last thought about Coaching Conversations. In Collaborative Workplaces, Coaching Conversations happen between managers and their direct reports. They also happen between coworkers, as peers work together to help each other learn and grow. That's why mastering the Coaching Conversation is essential for everyone.

BREAKTHROUGH TOOL:
THE STRAIGHT-TALK CONVERSATION SCRIPT

One of the most challenging conversations comes up when you have to approach a thorny subject with a coworker. How do you confront team members about problems, such as not delivering something as expected or even something personal such as wearing perfume or cologne that is too strong? Many people will do just about anything to avoid having these sorts of exchanges, and consequently, their problems never get solved. Or worse, they don't prepare for the conversation and end up sounding as if they are blaming others or accusing them of doing something wrong.

Many people say that they become more comfortable having a difficult conversation once it gets going. They just hate getting it started. Or they know if they don't start the conversation right, it can really go downhill fast. That's where the Straight-Talk Conversation tool can help. It gets a difficult conversation started in a productive way. A Straight-Talk Conversation combines candid words with a caring tone and is divided into four parts:

1. **Expectations.** If you haven't agreed upon expectations for the desired results or behaviors, it's difficult to tell people they're not meeting them. So you might have to begin there. If expectations are established, start by restating them. "As you know, the Sales Report is due on Fridays. One of our core values is accountability." Then...

2. **Observation.** State what you've observed, making it less about the person and more about the facts. The key is to use "I" statements rather than "you" statements. Instead of saying, "For at least the tenth time, you missed the deadline," say, "I received the report on Tuesday rather than by last Friday as we agreed."

3. **Impact.** Describe the outcome if the situation doesn't improve. "I see that the report was delivered on Tuesday rather than Friday as we agreed. I'm concerned because the president expects it on her desk on Tuesdays and my team has to rush to complete our part. I'm afraid she'll feel that we're not accountable if we miss the deadline."

4. **Offer to help.** Because this is a Collaborative Workplace, make it clear that you're not here to cast blame. You're here to help get the job done. This is the true spirit of collaboration. "As you know, the Sales Report is due on Fridays. One of our core values is accountability. I received the report on Tuesday rather than Friday as we agreed. I'm concerned because the president expects it on her desk on Tuesdays and my team has to rush to complete our part. I'm afraid she'll feel that we're not accountable if we miss the deadline. How can WE keep this from happening again?"

What is the *expectation?* What did I *observe?* What is the *impact?* How can I *help?* This Straight-Talk Conversation script gives you a simple, respectful way to bring difficult issues to the table. And don't forget to **follow up** by catching them doing it right the next time. It's a great way to reinforce the expectations while letting others know you're on the same team.

BREAKTHROUGH TOOL: THE AGREEMENT-BUILDING CONVERSATION SCRIPT

The third conversation framework is the Agreement-Building Conversation. Before you leave your next discussion or meeting, wouldn't it be nice if all of the parties involved walked away knowing everyone was on the same page, everyone has agreed to what was decided, and everyone knows the next steps? How often does that happen? Not very often. People wander around feeling confused and out of the loop—the telltale signs of a non-collaborative environment.

To develop agreement, build accountability, and foster consistency of message for your team, ask these four questions at the end of every meeting or discussion. Be sure to record the answers.

1. **What did we decide today?** This question helps to make sure that everyone is in complete agreement with the decisions that were made.

2. **Who is going to do what? By when?** These questions help to make sure that there is certainty around next steps and that a framework for accountability is established.

3. **Who needs to know about this?** This question ensures that everyone will be in the loop and no one will be left out, even those who aren't

part of the meeting or discussion. This is a critical question for improving communication and confidence in one another.

4. **What is the message and the tone of that message?** This question makes sure that everyone is on the same page and that all the people involved communicate with one voice.

At the conclusion of this Agreement-Building Conversation, everyone will be in alignment. All participants will be able to go back to their respective teams and relay the same message in a consistent way. And everyone who needs to know the decisions and next steps will be made aware of them.

Takeaway Tips:

○ A leading problem in most organizations is not a lack of communication. Rather, it's the inability to have collaborative conversations with one another.

○ The **Coaching Conversation**—*Tell me about...* (to really understand), *What ...?* (to set a goal), and *How ...?* (to create a plan)—guides and encourages others toward solving their own problems.

○ The **Straight-Talk Conversation**—observation, feeling, impact, offer to help—helps you and your coworkers confront difficult issues in a candid and caring way.

○ The **Agreement-Building Conversation**—What did we decide? Who is going to do what? By when? Who needs to know about this? What is the message and the tone of that message?—helps you and your teammates leave every meeting or discussion with clarity, purpose, direction, and the assurance that everyone will be kept in the loop.

CHAPTER 8

Commitment

If you want something from someone,
you can't just demand it.

You must give in order to get.

—*Mike Learner*

S ome days it's all about influence. You must influence your
direct reports to reach a certain level of performance. You
must influence others to see your way of thinking. You
even have to influence your boss to give you the resources to
implement your ideas.

But that's easier said than done, especially if you go about
it the way many people do: by making demands. Think about
what we typically do when we need something at work, say for

example, new software. We march into IT and declare, "I need new software by next month." And how does that go over with the IT team? Like a lead balloon.

Or let's imagine that you need your direct reports to pump out a large volume of work in a short period of time because your boss suddenly gives your department additional duties. If you do what many managers do in this situation, you call your team together and say something such as, "Okay guys, the boss has given us more work; therefore, we have no choice. Suck it up and get it done." You're not proactively influencing or managing anybody. You're simply making demands. Consequently, you're at the mercy of other people's whims. If the other department or your direct reports decide to derail your train, they can do it in a heartbeat.

FLASHBACK...

SHELLY'S PERSPECTIVE

Initially, I was shocked that Mike would go to Glinda about a reduction in benefits. I had just spent months overhauling our whole program at Glinda's direction so that people would feel better about working here and to attract the best job candidates. We hadn't had raises in two and a half years and, all of a sudden, Mike wants to dismantle the program? I thought, *What does he know about HR?* I shouldn't have been as defensive as I was in that e-mail, but I was exhausted and, quite frankly, frustrated that nobody appreciates what my team and I do. Still, I appreciated Mike's apology and his effort to bring us together to solve the problem. Talking it out in such a structured way allowed us to come up with a solution we could all commit to. It's too bad that Glinda didn't enlist Mike, Renaldo, Gina, and me from the beginning. It would have saved us a lot of time and aggravation had we known about the Gulfstream threat and been given the chance to work together to stop it. I believe that Mike will continue to work collaboratively with us as our new GM. He really deserves this opportunity.

Picture a team trying to come up with a strategy or solve a problem. Whose ideas do team members typically like the best? Each person thinks he or she has the right answer, but unfortunately, all the others think they have the right answers too. Conflict brews, decisions don't get made, and problems don't get solved because people can't agree on the right answer.

But a collaborative team knows that the right answer is not always the best answer. The best answer is the one that everyone can commit to. This doesn't mean that everyone has to agree in a unanimous way. Team members just need to commit. Getting people to commit requires dialogue and an opportunity for all team members to feel their opinions are heard. Getting people to commit is easier when others see their ideas reflected in the solution. Getting people to commit comes faster when people see how the solution benefits them.

Therefore, to influence others to commit to a solution or strategy, you have to take their interests into consideration. What's needed is a simple, surefire tool for building commitment in any group or one-on-one setting. That method is the **Five Questions.**

BREAKTHROUGH TOOL: THE FIVE QUESTIONS

The **Five Questions** will give you, your group, department, and/ or organization a broad range of information that can easily be distilled into your critical areas of focus. You will quickly know what to leverage, what to correct, what the barriers are, how others are willing to engage or provide resources, and where to start. The questions also create a tool for establishing better relationships with others, relationships that will lead to higher levels of commitment, influence, and collaboration.

1.   **What's working well?** This question starts the conversation on a positive note to surface the benefits of whatever you are examining. When you kick things off by making a list of all the things you do well (either as a team, organization, group, department, or as coworkers) it immediately becomes clear that this conversation is not an attack on anyone or anything. Now everyone can relax and be more receptive to the process.

2.   **What could we do better, differently, or more of?** This future- and solutions-oriented question introduces the need for change in a nonthreatening way. It gets people

focusing on possibilities, rather than dwelling on what's not working. As the suggestions start rolling in, think about what the ideas have in common so that you can begin grouping them into a few critical categories.

3.   **What is preventing the improvements identified in question number two?** This question uncovers any barriers to the suggested ideas and changes. People will begin to recognize obstacles that they didn't know existed before, thereby deepening their understanding of the real issues and constraints. Make a list of the barriers. Look for patterns, and focus on the critical few.

4.   **If only one change can be made, what should it be?** With this question, you show others that you're willing to understand their highest priority. When you can successfully tackle something that another person (especially a key person) wants, it signals that you're willing to help. You both will become energized and you can build on the momentum you've created. That's powerful mojo. Remember, this is all about nurturing better relationships, which will also help you influence more and gain commitment in the future. If you help people address their biggest priorities now, the next time you go knocking on their door, asking for something,

you'll have a better chance of their saying yes.

5.   **How can you help?** Asking others how they might help initiate change accomplishes three things. First, it opens people's eyes to the possibility that they themselves might have been a barrier to improvement up until now. Second, it allows you to begin developing a resource inventory based upon group and individual skills, talents, knowledge, ideas, and experiences. Third, it spotlights the necessity of teamwork. Sure, all team members are willing to share their ideas, but they also have to be willing to help. They can't just lay out all the things they want fixed without the expectation that they are part of both the problem and the solution. You have to work collaboratively to get things done. Question number five hammers home that concept.

The Five Questions put things in perspective. By the end of the inquiry, everybody will have direction, a vested interest, and some responsibility for what they need to do to move forward. You can use the Five Questions in many different situations:

1.   When you start working in a new position, use the Five Questions with your boss, peers, direct reports, other departments, and anyone who is willing to give you feedback about your new department or tasks. Their

answers will help you understand others' perceptions so you can set your goals and manage your priorities.

2. Use the Five Questions to identify ways to increase customer satisfaction with external and internal customers. One caveat: you would delete question number five when conducting a focus group with external customers. But you should definitely include it with internal customers. You never know how much they might be willing to help.

3. Create an employee survey using the Five Questions to identify employees' perceptions, likes, dislikes, and priorities for your work environment.

4. Use the Five Questions as a basis for an employee coaching session or performance review. Asking employees the Five Questions about their work and their on-the-job behavior helps them to identify their strengths and areas for improvement.

5. Send the Five Questions to a planning group prior to a planning session. If meeting participants take the time to think about their responses prior to the session, planning meetings will be full of constructive ideas and collaborative solutions.

Takeaway Tips:

○   Achieving aggressive goals and driving change in a fast-paced work environment takes full commitment from each team member.

○   Gaining commitment is about understanding and including others to build consensus and make decisions that leave everyone feeling excited and empowered.

○   The simplest, most effective method for building consensus and gaining commitment is to ask the **Five Questions:**

1.   What is working well?

2.   Would could we do better, differently, or more of?

3.   What is preventing the improvements identified in question number two?

4.   If only one change can be made, what should it be?

5.   How can you help?

○   Apply the **Five Questions** to evaluate projects, teams, or departments, and use them as a framework for customer and employee surveys, as a discussion guide for coaching sessions and performance reviews, or as preparation for a planning session.

CHAPTER 9

Clarity

Ideas make us feel good. Action makes us money.

—Mike Learner

When team members don't understand the future, they are forced to make assumptions and best-guess decisions, leaving far too much to chance. The workplace becomes cluttered with random ideas, competing goals, and conflicting priorities. What's the risk if your team lacks focus, clarity, or alignment of purpose? You end up long on ideas and short on execution. Or worse, good people make bad decisions. In business, the stakes are simply too high to allow that to happen. Yet, every day, organizations and the people within them muddle along without a clear understanding of the actions and behaviors all members must engage in to achieve their end goal. And that's a shame, because it's really not that difficult to get a team into alignment once you know how.

FLASHBACK...

JACK LEAPER'S PERSPECTIVE:

Each morning is a new opportunity to achieve something awesome. When an idea comes to mind, I like to grab onto it and put it into motion immediately. Action is important. If we run into roadblocks on the way, it's all right; pushing through them is part of the process. Time is of the essence. We can't give our competition the upper hand. Sometimes I am impatient with my team because they have trouble keeping up with me, and they don't understand the urgency when working in a global environment. I love it when they are engaged and enthusiastic when we work together. This kind of positive energy moves the company forward. I like Mike Learner's enthusiasm, and I'm glad he got me to create the Playbook. Our scoreboards look great and show everyone how successful we are. I am sure he'll keep those things in place as Lakeside's new GM. He can always call me to get more great ideas for taking this place to the next level.

THE CLARITY-BUILDING PROCESS

Whether the game is football, soccer, or hockey, every team has a playbook that contains the answers to the fundamental questions that everyone on the team must know in order to be successful. For example, let's imagine that you play for the Pittsburgh Steelers. If asked, **"What game do you play?"** what would your answer be? Come on, this isn't a trick question.

"We play football! Everyone on our team plays football," would be your response. It's as simple as that.

Then, if we asked, **"What championship are you trying to win?"** you'd say, "We are going to win the Super Bowl"—one big goal that everyone understands and gets excited about.

"And what will it take to win the Super Bowl?"

You could certainly reply that it takes teamwork, determination, and other admirable characteristics to win the world's biggest football game. But in its purest sense, to win the Super Bowl, you and the Steelers must win a number of regular season games so that you can make the playoffs. Then you must win those playoff games in order to get to the championship game. And if you win that big game, you and your teammates can proudly say, "We won the Super Bowl."

While you're playing those games, **how do you know whether you're winning or losing?** There's a scoreboard that tells you that. And the scoreboard is visible from the field throughout the game, so everyone on your team can consistently monitor whether the team is winning or not.

Here's a trickier question: **what differentiates your team from others?** There's a lot of football teams trying to win games so they can ultimately get to the Super Bowl. What differentiates the Pittsburgh Steelers from other teams? When you think of Pittsburgh, even with its beautiful rivers and cultural attractions, you think of the grit of its rough and tough steelworkers. In fact, the Pittsburgh Steelers have come to be known for "rough and tough" defense. Compare them to, say, the Dallas Cowboys. Love them or hate them, the Cowboys are all about flash, glitz, and their world-famous cheerleaders. That's what makes them unique and sets them apart from the rest.

In a nutshell, here is what's in the playbook of every football team:

o **What game do we play?** Football.

o **What championship are we trying to win?** The Super Bowl.

o **What will it take to win the championship?** We have to win games.

o **How will we keep score?** On the scoreboard.

o **What differentiates us from other teams?** In Pittsburgh's case, it's rough and tough defense.

Now let's translate this playbook concept to business because businesses with Collaborative Workplaces are also able to answer these same questions.

O   **What game do we play?** That's your mission or core purpose. Be sure it's simple and easy for people to remember.

O   **What championship are we trying to win?** That's your long-term vision. Be sure it's something everyone can get excited about.

O   **What will it take to win the championship?** You have to win games every day by achieving the goals you set for your organization.

O   **How will you keep score?** Through reports or displays that show outcomes, such as sales effectiveness, operating efficiencies, service indicators, financial reports, and the other measures you use every day.

O   **What differentiates us from other teams?** That definition is usually found in your core values or the beliefs and behaviors you expect people to bring to work and demonstrate throughout the day. These things become your brand and how you differentiate yourselves from the competition.

To recap, every team has a playbook, something that outlines the essential maneuvers to win the big game. No coach or player would operate without it. Yet, in business, we don't always take enough time to clearly outline goals and the key maneuvers it's going to take to achieve them. Whether you're a CEO responsible for an entire organization or a dedicated employee responsible for a small project, your Playbook is essential for your professional and personal success because it

○   clarifies your purpose for yourself and others;

○   creates a filter for decision making, resource allocation, and evaluating new opportunities;

○   helps you out-think the competition;

○   creates a common platform for change;

○   keeps you on track; and

○   puts the future in your control.

Do you have a Playbook? Maybe you call it a strategic plan, or perhaps you have scattered pieces here and there but nothing that pulls it all together. Think about it: Does every employee in your company know the answers to the Playbook questions? If we asked them what game your company plays, would they all be able to clearly express what you're about in just a few words? If we asked them what championship they are trying to win, would everyone answer with something as clear and simple as, "We're going to win the Super Bowl!"? Are your plays (goals) defined so clearly that all of your players know how they personally help to win games? Do you update your scoreboard in the work area every day so that people can measure their success or have an opportunity to self-correct if they are behind? Do they know your differentiators or the values that must shape their behaviors on the job?

People often overthink the elements of their Playbook and turn it into a lofty strategic plan and lengthy philosophical statements that are either too complicated for people to remember or are used by every other company in their industry. As a result, they lack inspiration and action orientation. You can avoid that by using the Playbook to create a clear and simple one-page plan to foster total clarity for you and your team.

BREAKTHROUGH TOOL: WRITING YOUR PLAYBOOK

The best plans are developed with a bit of research and a lot of input, so before you begin, research what's working and not working in your business (try using the **Five Questions** from the last chapter with your coworkers). Also share what's happening in your industry, your target markets, and your competitors' businesses.

Follow these simple steps to establish clarity, alignment, and a more focused and collaborative approach to your goals.

STEP 1

The motto in a Collaborative Workplace is "The more people know, the more they can contribute." Make it possible for all team members to contribute by first taking time to educate them on the essential elements of your business.

    a. **Customers:** Do they know who your best customers are? What makes a best customer? Is it profitability, volume, low service needs, cross-sell ratios, or some other factors? What steps do they need to take to create more "best customers"?

b. **Products:** What products and services do you offer? How do they work together and complement one another? What benefits do they bring to your customers?

c. **Competitors:** What do competitors do better than you do? What do you do better than your competitors? On what basis do you want to compete? How do you improve your competitive advantage?

d. **Industry and market trends:** What is happening in your industry? What are customers experiencing, and how does that influence their needs and demands?

e. **Financials:** How are you doing financially? How do you make money? What are your most significant revenue drivers? What drives costs?

STEP 2

Next, get the team together and ask our five Playbook questions:

1. **What game do we play?** This is your purpose or your mission. Notice that in the case of sports, only one word is necessary to define the game. Many mission statements drone on and on. Keep it simple (just a few words) so people know what your team does. It's okay that others do the same thing. Your differentiators will come from the next several questions. What is your mission?

2. **What championship are we trying to win?** This is your vision of what you hope to

achieve. Again, in the case of sports this is usually a single, simple, but very tangible outcome. Plus, it's something everyone can get excited about. In a business context, the championship might be bottom-line growth, market expansion, industry recognition, or an efficiency measure. What outcome or vision is everyone on your team shooting for?

3. **What must be achieved to win the championship?** These are the goals that must be achieved in order to win. In football, teams must win more games than other teams to get to the Super Bowl. The offense must score more goals. The defense must keep other teams from scoring. The field goal unit must get the ball through the uprights every time. The goals are clear to each team member. What goals must your team members achieve in order to attain your vision?

4. **How will we keep score?** This is how you keep score to make sure you are on target toward achieving your vision and goals. In football, a large scoreboard is visible by everyone in the stadium all throughout the game. The team doesn't wait for the next day's newspaper to see whether they won or lost. They know how they are doing every minute. Scoreboards display

the most important elements of the game and the ultimate measures of success. They are updated minute by minute as plays are made. How will you keep score?

5. **What differentiates us from other teams?** These differentiators are your core values. They define your image, workplace culture, and the behaviors your team must demonstrate to be successful in your organization. What are your organization's differentiators or values?

The answers to these questions are all it takes to create a Playbook that will guide your entire team's actions going forward. The answers to these questions can then be used to design marketing materials, employee expectations, operational practices, decision criteria, meeting frameworks, and more. Work with your team using this template to write your organization's Playbook. It builds purpose. It builds alignment. It builds clarity. It builds collaboration.

TEAM PLAYBOOK

OUR MISSION	OUR VISION
What game do we play?	What championship are we trying to win?

OUR VALUES

What differentiates us from other teams?

Goals: What must we achieve to win the championship?	Scoreboard: How will we keep score?	Who is responsible?	When will it be done?

Takeaway Tips:

- There are five Playbook questions all team members must be able to answer if they are to have total clarity: What game do we play? What championship are we trying to win? What must be achieved to win that championship? How will we keep score? What differentiates us from other teams?

- The best Playbooks are created after doing business and industry research and getting a lot of input from everyone on the team.

- The most effective Playbooks are brief (one page) and so simple that everyone can easily see how they contribute to the results.

CHAPTER 10

Courage

It's easier to ask for forgiveness
than to beg for permission.

—Mike Learner

Wherever you turn in life, you're likely to find some sort of problem that needs solving. Big problems, little setbacks, major difficulties, and minor snafus lurk around every corner. Nobody escapes this reality; everybody's up against one problem or another all the time.

To make ourselves feel better in this dynamic, problematic world, we try to put a positive spin on our difficulties by calling them "opportunities" and "challenges," yet no matter what you call them, they're problems. For some reason in our society, especially in the business arena, it's tough for people to admit they have problems and even tougher to tackle them.

Worse yet, people know problems exist, but they believe they are someone else's job to fix. They complain about the problems but wait for the solution to come from their boss, another department, or some other mysterious source. Organizations become stagnant when everyone sits around waiting for someone else to solve problems.

In a Collaborative Workplace, it's a wonderful thing when someone pipes up and declares a problem exists because that's the first step toward fixing it. Shining a light on problems is the mark of a true collaborator and perhaps a true leader: someone who confronts issues head on, takes initiative at the first sign of trouble, and is accountable for implementing solutions.

That's why it is critical to put your fears aside and ask yourself: **What's the most important or difficult issue that I need to solve right now?** You should always know the answer to that question and have the courage to start working on it as soon as you identify it. Don't be afraid to confront it. Don't be afraid to tackle it. Remember the final question that Marty always asked Mike Learner: **"What have you got to lose?"**

We suppose you could answer that question by saying, "Well gee, I could get fired, or people might think I'm being a pain in the neck." Of course, any number of painful things could happen. But is the fear of a bit of pain today enough to stop you from trying to make things better for yourself and your team for the long term?

Pointing out and tackling tough problems doesn't mean you have to be critical, especially if you take a respectful approach. It shows you're dedicated to busting through barriers and getting the job done right in a positive and professional way. Think about Lakeside's core values, the Three Rs: responsibility, respect, and results.

It's your personal and professional responsibility to look for problems, whether in yourself, your team, your department, or in the organization as a whole.

If you don't have **confidence** in someone, you must identify what's creating the lack of trust and figure out what you can do to improve it.

If you aren't having the right **conversations**, you must initiate them in order to enhance communication.

If your teammates don't have **commitment**, you must pull them together to work through the issues and resolve concerns.

If you don't have **clarity** in your work, you must create the Playbook to communicate your goals and priorities.

But don't forget **respect**. If you want to change the world, you have to change your thinking. With each interaction, you have to step back and ask why this person would want to talk to you. Have you earned his confidence? Do you have something meaningful that would add value to her work and life?

List what you know about your coworkers so you can determine what's important to them. How do you show that you respect their priorities? How do you speak their language by using words that show you care about those priorities too? After all, caring is one of the five Confidence Factors.

Once you start thinking differently, it's easy to collaborate more effectively with anyone. You can write your script for better conversations that build commitment and accountability. You can work together to create focused and disciplined teams that are innovative and successful. You can take action. And that's essential, because action is the only way you are going to get results.

FLASHBACK...

MIKE'S PERSPECTIVE:

Dr. Right, Glinda, and Jack had a lot of good qualities, but they weren't perfect. Working in the middle of the dysfunction was painful at times, but I know that people do things for a reason. So I did my best, and sometimes that meant keeping my head down and doing my best work. But there were also times when I felt I could make a difference.

Whenever that happened, I weighed the pros and cons of quitting versus staying and trying to make things better. I considered the potential consequences of those options and asked myself which of those two alternatives would make me feel better about myself in the long run. Truthfully, both alternatives were scary. If I quit, I'd have to start all over again somewhere else, and there were no guarantees that my new organization would be any better than Lakeside. If I stayed and tried to make Lakeside better, I risked ticking off key people or being labeled a troublemaker by my peers.

The thing that always sealed the deal for me was when I asked myself the question, "What have I got to lose?" When I considered all the angles, the only thing I had to lose was an unpleasant, ineffective workplace that made me regret having to get up in the morning—that and my self-respect. As a member of the Lakeside team, it was my responsibility to do everything in my power to make the organization the best it could be. If I abandoned ship in the middle of the storm without making an effort to bail some water, what would that say about me as an employee and a potential leader? What would that say about me as a person? In the end, I feel good about the decisions I made to collaborate with my peers and GMs. It was hard, but it was totally worth the risk and uncertainty. Even if it hadn't worked out as well as it did, at least I would have the satisfaction of knowing that I did my best to make it happen. And, if I can do it, I know you can too!

BREAKTHROUGH TOOL: DO YOU HAVE COURAGE?

Do you have a problem that's keeping you from reaping the benefits of a Collaborative Workplace? You have the power to address it right now. It just takes courage. If you are determined to create the kind of workplace where you can get things done and see the value of your contributions every day, while feeling rewarded and energized, then take the first step. Answer the questions below to build your action plan. Then get started!

What is the most difficult or important
issue I have to deal with right now?

_____

_____

_____

_____

To whom do I need to talk about this?

_____

_____

_____

Why would he/she want to talk to me?

_____

_____

_____

_____

What are his or her priorities?

_____

_____

_____

_____

How can I speak his or her language to
show that I care about his or her priorities?

_____

_____

_____

_____

Are there words I can use or actions I can
take to earn his or her confidence?

_____

_____

_____

_____

Which of the frameworks in this book can I use?

CONFIDENCE

☐ Confidence Quiz

☐ Confidence Inventory

☐ Team Confidence Inventory

CONVERSATIONS

☐ Coaching Conversation

☐ Straight-Talk Conversation

☐ Agreement-Building Conversation

COMMITMENT

☐ The Five Questions

CLARITY

☐ The Playbook

COURAGE

☐ Today is the day for your Collaboration Breakthrough. You already have everything you need to get the job done, so summon the courage to get out there and do it.

Because, honestly…**what have you got to lose?**

Learning to Speak Someone's Language

*To change the world, you first need
to change your thinking.*

Wow, what an exhilarating day! I'm still in shock that Jack's leaving and that I got to spend three hours with Charlene, the CEO. How often do you get a chance like that? And now I'm Lakeside's new general manager. When Charlene made the announcement later that day, my coworkers gave me a standing ovation. I was humbled beyond belief. I never thought I would be in this position.

Sure, I'm nervous about what's before me. I have to maintain the high level of energy and employee involvement that has given us the power to generate new ideas and grow the business. I also need to build more discipline around using the five Cs to make us more efficient and, more importantly, minimize the chaos the team currently feels. Adding structure and discipline is absolutely the way to move from our Open Workplace to a Collaborative Workplace. I know I can't eliminate all of the stress; it's just the way the world is. But with only a few simple tools, I'm confident we can get this team working more collaboratively than ever.

Before I wrap up for the day, though, I want to send out a few quick messages.

> To: Dr. Right
> From: Mike Learner
> Re: Thank you for your insight
>
> Dr. Right:
>
> I am not sure if you heard, but I have been promoted to the general manager's position at Lakeside. I would like to thank you for showing me how important it is to have the courage to make tough decisions and to maintain a constant focus on the quality of our products and processes. I will remember your excellent example as I move forward. I appreciate your confidence in me and I wish you continued success.

To: Glinda Nuturino
From: Mike Learner
Re: Thank you for your support

Dear Glinda:

I am not sure if you've heard, but I've been promoted to the general manager's position at Lakeside. Thank you for showing me how important it is for our team members to work well together. I will remember this as I move forward. I hope you're enjoying your retirement. Please send me some pictures of you and your grandchildren when you have time.

To: Jack Leaper
From: Mike Learner
Re: Thank you for your inspiration

Hey Jack:

Sorry you had to rush off so quickly today. I just wanted to shoot you a quick e-mail to thank you for being such an inspiring leader and coach. I would like to thank you for showing me the importance of getting the team energized around new ideas. I will remember this as I move forward. I hope you score big as the VP of Global Sales!

Dr. Right, Glinda, and Jack may have had their faults, but who doesn't? Come to think of it, my most important lesson was learning how to figure each of them out. I had to learn what was important to them and how to speak their language to be sure my voice was heard. Had Marty not been there for me in the moments when I was most frustrated, I would never have learned that. I would have quit a long time ago.

When Marty first asked me, "How do you speak his language?" I had no idea what he was talking about. But over time, it became perfectly clear.

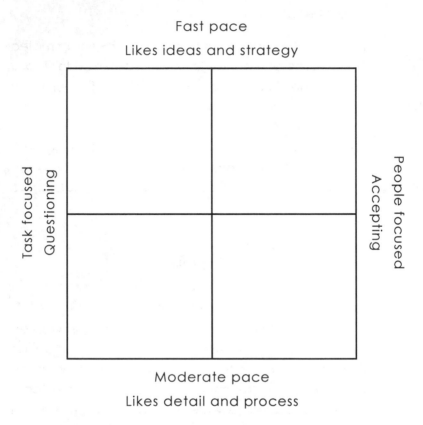

Some people tend to be fast-paced, big-picture thinkers. Other people tend to be more moderately paced because they think about details and processes.

Some people like to focus on tasks and have a more questioning nature, whereas others are more people oriented and have a more accepting nature. When you combine these things, you can really figure people out.

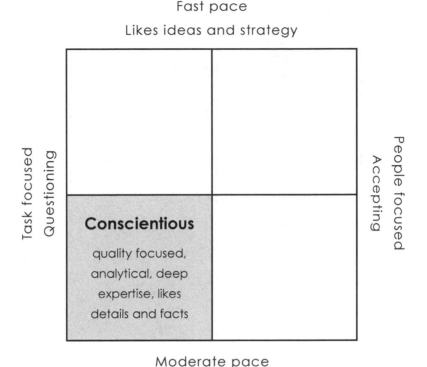

There's no doubt that Dr. Right was into the details. He definitely was not people oriented. But he was one of the most Conscientious people I have ever known. His top priority was quality. He valued expertise and a fact-based, logical approach to decision making. Sure, he could take a long time to make decisions, and he would do so without including others, but I think that was because he was so afraid of being wrong. Once I earned his confidence by showing him that I knew my facts and that I valued quality too, I got along with him just fine. Others who didn't figure this out weren't so lucky.

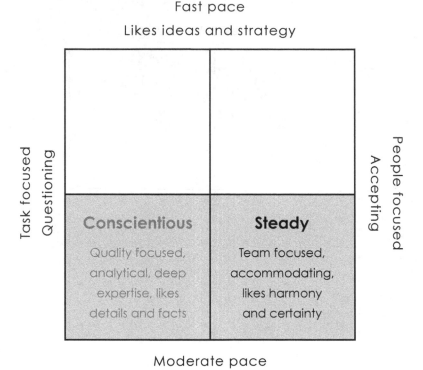

Fast pace
Likes ideas and strategy

Task focused
Questioning

People focused
Accepting

Conscientious

Quality focused,
analytical, deep
expertise, likes
details and facts

Steady

Team focused,
accommodating,
likes harmony
and certainty

Moderate pace
Likes detail and process

Then there was Glinda. As was Dr. Right, she was cautious and thoughtful in her approach but for different reasons. She was much more people oriented, and she wanted us to get along and cooperate with one another. She was really the picture of Steadiness. Her top priority was maintaining a harmonious work environment. She valued teamwork and serving others. She hated conflict, but I think it was because she was afraid of instability and uncertainty. Once I got my peers together to hash through our differences and present a unified front, Glinda felt comfortable enough to support almost every recommendation we came up with.

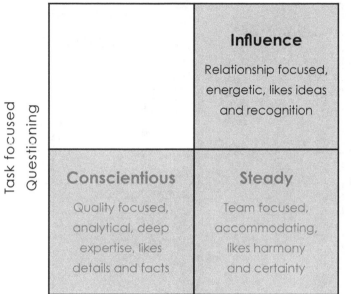

Fast pace
Likes ideas and strategy

Influence

Relationship focused, energetic, likes ideas and recognition

Conscientious

Quality focused, analytical, deep expertise, likes details and facts

Steady

Team focused, accommodating, likes harmony and certainty

Task focused
Questioning

People focused
Accepting

Moderate pace
Likes detail and process

And then there was Jack, the ultimate people person. He was full of energy and enthusiasm for any new idea that might help him achieve his big picture goals. I'd call him high in Influence. His top priority was pioneering new ideas. He loved selling his ideas and getting people excited about them. Because he was so impulsive, he often needed us to take care of the details for him. But we followed through because we knew it was so important to him that we looked good—okay, that *he* looked good. Once I showed him how writing a Playbook would give us more focus—and also make him the MVP of the game—he was more than willing to give it a try.

Fast pace
Likes ideas and strategy

Dominant Results focused, direct, authoritative, fast decision maker, likes to win	**Influence** Relationship focused, energetic, likes ideas and recognition
Conscientious Quality focused, analytical, deep expertise, likes details and facts	**Steady** Team focused, accommodating, likes harmony and certainty

Task focused
Questioning

People focused
Accepting

Moderate pace
Likes detail and process

Last but not least was Charlene. Like Jack, she was a big-picture thinker who moved at lightning speed. But I got the sense that her top priority was not about looking good to others but, rather, excellent results and the bottom line. She wanted to achieve big things quickly. I'd call her Dominant. She is direct and wants to win. She is motivated by power and authority and probably fears losing control. Since I'll be reporting to her going forward, I'll need to be respectful of her position and be proactive in showcasing that we are exceeding our goals and beating the competition.

This was why Marty's insights into human nature were so brilliant. He knew that business isn't just about numbers. It's also about psychology. He helped me to appreciate each of my boss's strengths, to change my perspective, and to think about what would be important to each of them. Then he helped me to adapt my conversations with them to speak their language. I didn't always get what I wanted, but I always felt that my voice was heard and that conversations were mutually beneficial. Plus, with each conversation, relationships were strengthened. Speaking their language brought our different perspectives, styles, and approaches together, helping us move closer to achieving a Collaborative Workplace. I couldn't have done any of this without Marty. I decided I ought to find him so I could thank him.

Just then, Shelly appeared at my door.

"I just wanted to stop by and give you my personal congratulations," she said with a warm smile. "I'm really happy for you, Boss. Actually, I'm happy for all of us. I have a feeling that great things are really going to start happening around here."

"Thanks, Shelly," I replied, "but you don't have to call me boss. In fact, I kind of like just being Mike. You're as important around here as I am; we just sit in different chairs."

It dawned on me that Shelly was probably a combination of Conscientiousness and Steadiness. She worked super hard on the details and processes of our human resources functions. She was really angry when I questioned her expertise and hard work on the benefits changes, but she came around quickly when we took a collaborative and structured approach to working through our disagreements.

It also occurred to me that being head of HR, Shelly could probably point me in the right direction to find Marty.

"Shelly, there's someone I really want to talk to. Do you know where I might find Marty from the mailroom?"

"Who?"

"Marty, the older gentleman who works at night delivering mail to people's desks."

"Mike, all of today's excitement must be getting to you. We don't have a mailroom. We get so little snail mail these days that the front desk processes it all. And I can assure you that no one named Marty works here. As VP of HR, I know everyone here, where they work, and everything about them, professionally and personally."

Well, that was confirmation of Shelly's Conscientious, thorough style for sure. But what was she saying? No one named Marty worked here? There was no mailroom? The front desk processed it all? Now that I had stopped to think about it, Marty never actually gave me any mail.

Maybe the excitement of the day's events had gotten to me after all. Or maybe, just maybe, I'd already known, deep down, everything "Marty" had told me. During what I thought was my first "conversation" with him, he told me I already had everything it took to be successful here at Lakeside. Maybe I just needed all those challenging moments to force me to look at people differently. To change the world, you first have to change your thinking. In order to influence my bosses and coworkers, I first had to change my perspective. I had to understand and appreciate them as individuals and apply one of my five Cs to build a Collaborative Workplace.

In fact, these ideas aren't all that novel. They're really just common sense. So perhaps the real secret to our success here at Lakeside is in *how we work together*. We proactively build *confidence* in one other. We have great *conversations*. We address people's viewpoints and concerns to build *commitment*. We align with *clarity* based on what's in our Playbook. We have the *courage* to tackle the most important or difficult issues. We're creating solutions that everyone feels good about. We're getting results that everyone is proud of. We're maintaining an environment where people are energized by their work. In short, we're creating a Collaborative Workplace.

And this time, it's not a dream.

Acknowledgments

For some, courage comes from within. For me, courage comes from the many people with whom I've had the honor of working over the years. They have inspired me, challenged me, cheered for me, and encouraged me to think big, create magic, and achieve more. For them, I owe my deepest thanks.

To our amazing clients, whom we constantly try to follow from two steps ahead. Your successes have proven the benefits of a Collaborative Workplace. Your challenges have led to the five C's and the simple tools in this book. We are grateful for your business, your inspiration, and your friendships.

To the Western New York community, you have given us a platform upon which to build our business and share our beliefs. We are proud to be part of our wonderful resurgence and hope we can continue to give back.

To our world-class tool providers, we are honored to represent your assessments and training programs. The solutions from Wiley, the Center for Applied Cognitive Studies, Performance Support Systems, and Unboxed allow us to make our customers say, "Wow!" every day.

To the hardworking team who made this book a reality, we've talked about this for a long time. But without you, it would have never happened. Many thanks to Pamela Suarez, Erin Johnson, Tina Smagala, and Alaina Oleston, as well as the collaborative team at Advantage Media Group.

To the amazing Work Ignited team, Stephanie Phibbs and Kris Coleman, we have climbed many mountains and hiked through many valleys together. But, there are no better collaborators and friends that I would want by my side.

To our families and friends, we are eternally grateful for your never-ending support as we took some risks to chase our dreams.

"Where there is no guidance, a people falls,
but in an abundance of counselors there is safety."

—Proverbs 11:14

About the Author

How could just one person write a book about collaboration? Knowing that would be impossible, Amy Pearl and the dynamic team at Work Ignited...well...collaborated. Together, they provide strategic solutions and simple tools to ignite your passion, ignite your team, and ignite your workplace.

For over two decades, Amy and her team have built Collaborative Workplaces of all shapes and sizes across North America. They specialize in:

- employee surveys to measure the level of collaboration in your workplace;

- online micro-learning to put knowledge, training, coaching, mentoring, career development, and community learning right at your team's fingertips;

- Lead Ignited, a robust development program to build your leadership talent; and

- speaking engagements to energize your team.

Amy and the Work Ignited team share a passion for family and having fun at work, and their energy and enthusiasm is contagious. The team believes strongly in giving back. A portion of the proceeds from this book will be used to promote and advance behavioral and emotional health in the Western New York community.

Interested in collaborating with Amy and the Work Ignited team? Contact them at 716-276-8005 or visit www.CollaborationBreakthrough.com.

Create your
COLLABORATION BREAKTHROUGH
Today

Visit **CollaborationBreakthrough.com** to get the resources you
need to be a collaborative force in your organization.

FREE RESOURCES

www.CollaborationBreakthrough.com to take
our Workplace quiz and get other free stuff!

COLLABORATION BREAKTHROUGH
E-COURSE

Create a Collaboration Breakthrough in your life with
this 60 minute online learning program. You'll start by
identifying your current and ideal workplace. Then,
you'll get tools and tips that go beyond what's in
this book to create a Collaborative Workplace and
achieve your goals. Volume discounts allow your
entire team to get up to speed on our Breakthrough
Tools quickly, easily and cost-effectively.

SPEAK THEIR LANGUAGE WITH
EVERYTHING DISC®

In just 15 minutes, you can have the knowledge and
tools to communicate effectively with any one at any
level. First, you'll take the Everything DiSC Workplace
Profile. Once complete, you'll receive your Profile and
our *Speak Their Language Starter Kit* to create a road
map for communicating with everyone in your life.

CREATING A COLLABORATIVE WORKPLACE SURVEY AND INTERACTIVE TEAM EXPERIENCE

Identify which workplace exists at your organization and become a more collaborative team. Our employee survey is quick to administer and yields dozens of actionable ideas for increasing your level of collaboration. In our interactive team experience, you and your coworkers will review your survey results and roll up your sleeves to work together to build your action plan and commitment to success.

GET CERTIFIED

Are you an HR professional, coach or consultant interested in delivering our *Creating a Collaborative Workplace Interactive Team Experience* in your organization or for your clients? Our Facilitation Kit includes scripts, participant guides, presentations, videos, experiential activities, and the supplies you need to wow your audience while getting results. Build your skills, increase your network and make yourself more marketable by attending our two-day Get Certified Workshop.

SPEAKING ENGAGEMENTS

Give your audience the opportunity to have a Collaboration Breakthrough while getting the tools to solve their most important or difficult problems. Author Amy Pearl or another member of the team will light up your audience and give them the courage to make it happen.

Printed in the USA
CPSIA information can be obtained
at www.ICGtesting.com
JSHW011417160824
R13664500003B/R136645PG68134JSX00038B/19